STUDY SKILLS TO THE RESCUE!

Written by
Jan Brennan

Editor
Joellyn Thrall Cicciarelli

Illustrator
Karl Edwards

Designer
Moonhee Pak

Project Director
Carolea Williams

TABLE OF CONTENTS

4 **INTRODUCTION**

7 **ORGANIZATION**

How Organized Are You?
The Desk Inspector
The Bedroom Inspector
Personal Study Style
Eyes on Supplies
Pick a Place for Homework
Creating a Book Cover
Organizing Paperwork
Filing Completed Work
No More Homework Excuses
Study Buddy
Minimizing Distractions
Double-Checking Your Work

21 **TIME MANAGEMENT**

How Well Do You Use Your Time?
Prioritizing
Track Your Time
Cool Calendar
Weekly Planner
Homework Grid
Step by Step
Time Judge
Time-Savers
Taking Breaks

37 **READING STRATEGIES**

Can You Find & Remember Information When You're Reading?
Preparing to Read
Reading a Paragraph
Reading a Textbook Chapter
Scanning
Skimming
SQ3R
Reading Novels

49 **TAKING NOTES**

Are You a Good Note-Taker?
Taking Notes as You Read
Taking Notes as You Listen
Note-Taking Short Cuts
Asking Questions for Better Notes
Creating an Outline from Your Notes
Writing Your Own Outline
Using Your Notes

61 **ORAL PRESENTATIONS**

How Well Do You Give an Oral Presentation?
Getting the Facts
Outline for a Speech
Preparing an Oral Presentation
Public-Speaking Tips
Adding Fun Elements

69 **REPORTS & THE WRITING PROCESS**

Are You a Precise, Efficient Report Writer?
Getting the Facts
Prewriting
Using Reference Materials
Preparing Note Cards
Making an Outline from Note Cards
Rough Drafts
Editing
Final Drafts
Finishing Touches

81 **MEMORY BUILDERS**

Do You Have a Good Memory?
Acronyms
Acrostics
Pictures in Your Mind
Drawing Sketches
Flip Books
Songs
Rhymes
Time Lines
Remembering Dates with Rhymes
Remembering Numbers
Group Games

93 **TEST PREPARATION**

Do You Know How to Study for a Test?
Game Plan
Studying Alone
Studying with a Partner
Studying in a Group

99 **TEST-TAKING SKILLS**

Are You a Good Test-Taker?
Underlining Key Words
Reading Test Directions
Checking Math Tests
Matching Tests
Multiple-Choice Tests
True-or-False Tests
Fill-in-the-Blank Tests
Essay Tests

109 **PARENT LETTERS**

111 **ANSWER KEY**

INTRODUCTION

Study Skills to the Rescue! provides a wealth of resources, ideas, and activities to help your students become better learners—students who know how to gain and apply knowledge to the best of their ability.

Through fun, easy-to-implement activities, your students will learn how to

- become organized.
- effectively manage their free time and homework time.
- use valuable reading strategies such as SQ3R.
- take notes.
- prepare and write outstanding reports.
- prepare and present oral presentations.
- improve memory-building techniques.
- prepare for and take tests to the best of their ability.

Study Skills to the Rescue! uses "friendly" language that all upper-grade students can relate to. And as your students learn study skills in this comfortable way, they will

- discover how they learn best.
- prepare for the transition to higher levels of learning.
- learn to make intelligent decisions about how to complete assignments and commit information to memory.

This comprehensive collection of student activities incorporates a variety of study skills. Each activity has been specially developed so students can follow the directions independently. But it is also important that you read and understand the sheets before reproducing and presenting them.

Each section of *Study Skills to the Rescue!* begins with a reproducible survey so students can self-evaluate their development in a specific study-skill area, such as organization. You can have students complete and discuss a survey each time you introduce a new skill.

The activities that follow the surveys are presented in an easy-to-use format. Introductory information is presented first to help students understand why a specific study skill is important. Activity directions follow the introductory information. The activities invite students to use their thinking skills, best judgment, and imagination to learn and then transfer study skills to everyday life. Each activity asks students to record their learning so you have a written record of their progress and accomplishments. Each activity offers a study buddy tip—valuable information that relates to the study skill in the activity. An answer key is provided on pages 111–112 to help you check student work.

ARE YOU A PRECISE, EFFICIENT REPORT WRITER?

Name

Directions

Read each statement and circle a number from 0–4. Total your points and check your score at the bottom to see how well you write reports.

1. I ask my teacher the "right" questions to find out the requirements for a report.
2. I know how to gather facts from books and computers for my report.
3. I brainstorm before I write.
4. I organize report facts on note cards and in an outline.
5. I carefully write my rough draft.

Getting the Facts

Name

Directions

Read the report description and answer the questions on this page and page 71. Keep this page so you can ask the same questions when you are assigned a "real" report.

Report Description for Reading Class

You have been assigned to write a report about a favorite athlete. It is due two weeks from today's date. The report should be at least three pages long. The report can be handwritten or typed. It should be single spaced with a double space between paragraphs. Page numbers should appear at the bottom center of each page. The report should be placed in a folder and should include at least one illustration. You should have a bibliography with at least two sources.

1. In which class has the report been assigned? ________
2. What is the subject of the report? ________
3. When is the report due? ________
4. What form of writing should be used?
   a. handwritten
   b. typed
   c. handwritten or typed
   d. other ________

The activities can be presented in any order and should be used in a way that best meets your students' needs. Don't feel like you have to present all the activities; pick and choose the ones that work best. The following are just a few ways to present the activities:

- Designate the first month of school as "Study Skills Month." Teach all study skills within the first month of school to prepare students for the upcoming year.
- Teach one study skill each month, presenting all sheets in specific sections as comprehensive units.
- Use a section's activities when presenting an assignment or a test that requires students to use a new study skill.
- Use only the activities that apply to the class(es) you are currently teaching.
- If you teach a class dedicated to study skills, read the activities, choose those that correlate with your curriculum, and get started!

Introduce, implement, and close each activity with plenty of class discussion. The activities are meant to be a springboard for meaningful interaction between you and the students to help them understand your expectations regarding study skills. In addition, some of the vocabulary will be new to your students—they will need your guidance and classroom discussion to learn the new words.

To "bring the learning home," two informative parent letters are provided on pages 109 and 110. These letters strengthen the home–school connection and emphasize the importance of helping children with homework and time management.

With the terrific activities in each section of this book, your students can learn to meet and exceed your and their expectations for learning, remembering, and using their knowledge in school. So get started today—it's *Study Skills to the Rescue!*

HOW ORGANIZED ARE YOU?

A big part of doing well in school is being ready to do well. Are you always ready? Take the following survey to find out.

Name ______________________________

Directions

Read each statement and circle a number from 0–4. Total your points and check your score at the bottom to see how organized you are.

0 = never   1 = occasionally   2 = sometimes   3 = often   4 = always

	Statement					
1	I keep my desk/locker neat and in order.	0	1	2	3	4
2	My bedroom is neat and everything has a place.	0	1	2	3	4
3	I have all the supplies I need to do my work in class.	0	1	2	3	4
4	I have all the supplies I need to do my homework.	0	1	2	3	4
5	I have a system to organize my papers.	0	1	2	3	4
6	I have an at-home study area without distractions.	0	1	2	3	4
7	I double-check my work.	0	1	2	3	4
8	I do important tasks first.	0	1	2	3	4
9	I remember to do and bring in my homework.	0	1	2	3	4
10	I know how I learn and study best.	0	1	2	3	4
11	I save my completed work in case I need it later.	0	1	2	3	4

If you scored

- **40 or above,** *congratulations! Watch out for some new tips to help you become even more organized!*
- **27–39,** *you're almost there. Be ready to learn some new tips to bring up your score.*
- **14–26,** *you need some help getting organized. The upcoming tips will really help you.*
- **0–13,** *it's time to get organized! Be ready to learn some important organization tips!*

Name ______________________________

The Desk Inspector

When you can find things in your desk or locker, you can complete your work well and on time.

______________________'s Desk or Locker   Inspected by: ______________________

Directions

Inspect a partner's desk or locker and complete the checklist. Have your partner do the same for your desk or locker. Then read the grades you were given and make a list of ways you can improve the condition of your desk or locker.

Area and Grading Scale	Circle the grade for the area. (Write three examples to support each grade.)
Desktop (skip if inspecting a locker) A = open area D = total clutter	A B C D • • •
Inside of Desk or Locker A = neat and organized D = too full, messy	A B C D • • •
Supplies A = everything he or she needs D = hardly any	A B C D • • •
Distractions A = no distractions D = lots of personal items, such as food or toys	A B C D • • •

Be sure to clean out your desk or locker at least once a month.

Name ______________________________

The Bedroom Inspector

Having a neat bedroom can help you sleep better, study better, and find what you need right away.

Directions

For homework, inspect each listed bedroom area and circle the number that shows how well it is organized. Then follow the directions under each area's description. Have a family member sign the bottom of this page.

Set aside one day each week to clean up your room.

Inspect the following bedroom areas:

Bookshelves crammed full **0** **1** **2** **3** neat and organized

(If you scored below a 2, sort through your books, donate old or unused ones, and reshelve your books in alphabetical order.)

Drawers full and cluttered **0** **1** **2** **3** neat and organized

(If you scored below a 2, take out outgrown clothes, organize remaining clothes, arrange nonclothing drawers, and throw away clutter.)

Closet overflowing **0** **1** **2** **3** neat and organized

(If you scored below a 2, take out outgrown clothes, hang up clothes, and put your shoes in pairs.)

Floor covered with junk **0** **1** **2** **3** clear

(If you scored below a 2, pick up all stray items and find a place for them, rearrange furniture for more space, and vacuum.)

Under Bed cluttered **0** **1** **2** **3** neat and organized

(If you scored below a 2, clean out all items and place them in labeled boxes.)

______________________________ completed this assignment.
(student's name)

____
(family member's signature)

Name ______________________

Personal Study Style

Everyone has a way he or she studies best—a personal study style.
If you can recognize and use it, you will be more successful when you study.

Directions

Read each statement and circle the answer to show what helps you most. Then meet with a partner and explain how your study habits should change to best match your personal study style.

1. I remember directions to a friend's house best when he or she
   - **a.** tells them to me. (auditory learner)
   - **b.** writes them down. (visual learner)
   - **c.** walks there several times with me. (kinesthetic learner)

2. The best time for me to study is
   - **a.** the first thing in the morning.
   - **b.** right after school.
   - **c.** before bedtime.

3. I study best when I study
   - **a.** alone.
   - **b.** with a partner.
   - **c.** in a group.

4. I concentrate best when there is
   - **a.** no noise at all.
   - **b.** background noise.

5. The best position for me to study in is
   - **a.** at a desk or table.
   - **b.** on the floor.

6. I like the room where I study to be
   - **a.** warm.
   - **b.** cool.

Show this survey to your family and ask them to help you create a home study area that matches your study style.

Name ______________________________

Eyes on Supplies

To be the best student you can be, you need the right supplies for all your subjects.

Directions

List your subjects in the first column. Read the supply ideas in the second column and cross out those you already have. Think about your subjects and write a shopping list in the third column. Include supplies from the second column and anything else you need.

School Subjects

1. ______________________
2. ______________________
3. ______________________
4. ______________________
5. ______________________
6. ______________________
7. ______________________

Supply Ideas

- backpack
- 3-ring binder
- calculator
- colored pencils
- crayons
- pens
- pencils
- erasers
- construction paper
- folders
- writing paper
- typing paper
- index cards
- hole punch
- glue
- markers
- paper clips
- pencil sharpener
- ruler
- scissors
- spiral notebook
- stapler
- correction fluid
- tape

Shopping List

____
____
____
____
____
____
____
____
____
____
____
____
____
____
____
____
____

STUDY BUDDY TIP: If you have brothers and sisters, set up an at-home "supply station" where you keep supplies that can be shared.

Name ______________________________

Pick a Place for Homework

Where you study can affect how long you spend on homework and how well you complete it. Try to find a place at home where you can do your best work.

Directions

Read and answer the questions. Discuss your answers with a partner. Draw a picture on page 13 to show the at-home study area that's best for you.

If you have trouble finding a good study space at home, ask a parent or adult friend to take you to the library.

1. In what room do you currently study? ______________________________
2. Do you study in the same place every day? ______________________________
3. Do you study on the floor, at a table, on your bed, or at a desk? ______________________________
4. Is that the best place for you? __________
5. Are all the supplies you need right at your fingertips? __________
6. Can you concentrate in this area? __________ Why or why not? ______________________________
____
7. Is the noise level in your study area right for you? __________
8. Is your study area well lit? __________
9. Is your study area comfortable? __________
10. What distractions, if any, are in your study area? ______________________________
____
11. Do you need to make a change in your study area? __________
If so, where might be a better place for you to study? ______________________________
12. If you are going to continue studying in the same place, how can you make the area better?
____
____

Name ______________________________

Directions

Talk about the questions you answered on page 12 and then draw a picture of your ideal study area.

Name ______________________________

Creating a Book Cover

Book covers save books from wear and tear, and you can record information on them to turn them into great organizational tools.

1. Open the book you want to cover and lay it on a table. Cut a large paper grocery bag so it is 6" (15 cm) wider and 4" (10 cm) longer than the book.

2. Place the plain side of the bag down, open the book, and place it in the middle of the bag. There will be 3" (7.5 cm) of bag showing on either side of the book and 2" (5 cm) of bag showing at the top and bottom.

3. Fold and crease the bag along the book's top and bottom edges. Remove the book and fold the top and bottom edges flat.

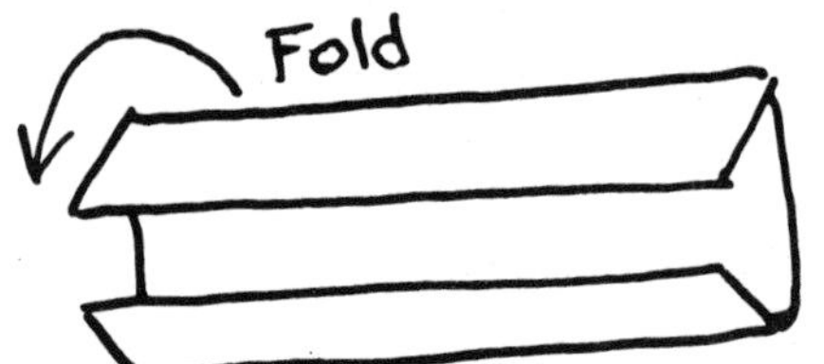

4. Place the open book in the center of the cover. Fold the right side of the bag in to the edge of the book to form a sleeve. Slip the right end of the book into the sleeve and tape it to the top and bottom of the bag without taping the book.

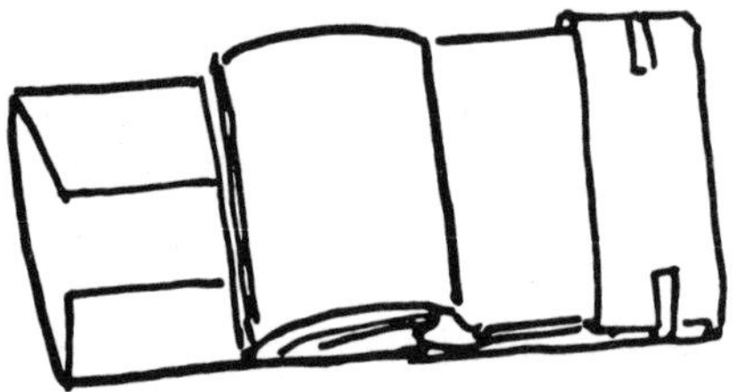

5. Fold the left side of the bag into the edge of the book to form a sleeve. Slip the left end of the book into the left sleeve and close the book. (If you don't close the book, the cover will be too small.) Lift the cover slightly and tape the left sleeve to the top and bottom of the cover.

6. Use crayons or markers to label and decorate the front cover. Leave the back cover blank and use it to record test dates or homework reminders.

Study Buddy Tip: Don't forget to write the book title on the cover and on the spine so you can find the book on a shelf!

Name ______________________________

Organizing Paperwork

It's important to have an organized system for your paperwork so you know what and where your assignments are and how and when to complete them.

Directions

Read the paperwork plans. Choose the one that will work best for you; then answer the questions.

Clean out your folders/binder at the end of each grading period. Keep and file important papers. Recycle the rest.

	Plan 1: Folders	Plan 2: Three-Ring Binder
What	• different-colored folder for each subject • extra one for notices, planner, calendar, and supply list	• different folder and divider for each subject • other folders for notices, planner, calendar, and supply list
How to Use	• loose-leaf paper and assignments in right pocket • handouts and notes in left pocket • label each folder with your name, teacher's name, and room number	• loose-leaf paper in rings • each subject's assignments, handouts, and notes in a different folder • label divider between each folder with subject and room number • label binder with your name
Advantages	• inexpensive • lightweight • color-coded • can carry as many or as few as you wish	• everything is in one place • only have to remember to bring one thing • durable • can hold a lot
Disadvantages	• easy to lose one • not durable • cannot hold a lot	• more expensive than folders • can become heavy and disorganized • you can lose everything

1. Which plan will work best for you? ______________________________
2. Why? ______________________________

____

3. By what date will your plan be in place? ____________________

Name ______________________________

Filing Completed Work

Don't throw away those old papers! Instead, file them so you have the information for later reference and to study for tests.

Directions

Complete the following directions to create a filing system for your paperwork. Check off each direction as you finish, and have a family member sign at the bottom of this paper to show that you created a filing system.

_______ **1** Use one file folder for each subject. Label each folder with the name of the subject, such as math, reading, spelling, language arts, social studies, science, or art.

_______ **2** Place the folders in a convenient, central location, such as a deep desk drawer or large box.

_______ **3** Tonight and every night from now on, file completed papers in the appropriate folder. Be sure a date is on each paper.

Clean out the folders at the end of each grading period. Before throwing away any papers, ask your teacher if there is anything you should save for future reference. Keep large projects, such as research reports, and any work you are especially proud of.

From time to time, look back at your old papers. You'll feel really proud when you notice how much you've learned!

______________________________ has created a filing system for his/her paperwork.
(student's name)

____
(family member's signature)

Name ____________________

No More Homework Excuses

Making a plan to complete and bring in your homework is almost as important as getting it done. You don't want your teachers to miss seeing that great work!

Directions

Pretend you are the student in each story and write how you would do things differently. Then meet with a group to discuss the answers.

Alana sat down in class, opened her folder, and discovered that her homework wasn't there! She had left it on the kitchen table and both her parents were already at work. When her name was called, Alana said that she had her paper, but someone had stolen it. Alana asked for credit because it wasn't her fault that the work was missing.

Where did Alana go wrong? What would you do to avoid her problem?

____

____

____

____

Juan got home from school, made himself a snack, and opened his backpack to begin his homework. As Juan read a worksheet, he discovered that he needed his textbook to complete it. Juan had left his textbook in his locker.

Where did Juan go wrong? What would you do to avoid his problem?

Brenden had soccer, scouts, and video-game time every day, so he put off a big report until the morning it was due. When he couldn't complete it in time, Brenden pretended to be sick so he could stay home.

Where did Brenden go wrong? What would you do to avoid his problem?

Let your parents, brothers, or sisters know about your homework. They can help you complete it and remind you to turn it in.

Name ______________________

Study Buddy

It's always good to have a friend to help you with homework, remind you to turn it in, and become your "homework delivery service" if you're sick.

Directions

Team up with a friend who lives near you. Make an agreement that you'll help each other with homework, share books if necessary, and deliver homework to each other when one of you is sick. Complete the certificate showing who your study buddy is and how you will help him or her.

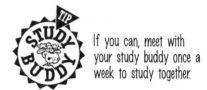

If you can, meet with your study buddy once a week to study together.

STUDY BUDDY

Date: ______________________

I, ______________________,
(your name)

agree to help ______________________
(partner's name)

with homework in ______________________,
(name of subject or class)

to share books, and to bring homework to his or her house in case of illness.

____
(your signature)

Name ______________________________

Minimizing Distractions

If you know how to keep distractions to a minimum, you'll concentrate better when you're studying.

Directions

Think about each distraction. If it stops you from studying, circle it. If it doesn't distract you, cross it out. Then try the suggestions next to each circled item.

Distractions You Can See	What You Can Do
1. Television	Turn it off.
2. Computer game	Turn it off.
3. Other people	Leave the room or close the door.
4. Toys and other games	Put them away.
5. Bright or "busy" objects	Put them away.

Distractions You Can Hear	What You Can Do
6. Telephone	Use an answering machine, turn off the ringer, or close the door.
7. Television	Turn it off.
8. Radio	Turn it off.
9. People talking	Politely ask people to speak quietly.
10. Computer	Turn it off or leave the room.

Distractions You Can Feel	What You Can Do
11. Hungry	Get a snack.
12. Tired	Take a break, get some fresh air, or exercise.
13. Bored	Take a break.

Are you distracted by anything else? Think about it and write your ideas below.

Other Distractions	What I Can Do
______________________	______________________
______________________	______________________
______________________	______________________
______________________	______________________
______________________	______________________

If noise really bothers you, put on a headphone set and listen to "dead air"!

Name ______________________________

Double-Checking Your Work

It's important to double-check your work for mistakes, even if you've completed your work carefully.

Directions

Pretend the report below is yours. Double-check the report for mistakes. Underline each mistake. Meet with a partner and talk about the mistakes you found. Share your findings with the class to see how well you did.

Challenge yourself to find 100 mistakes when you double-check a week's worth of work. Reward yourself with computer time or a snack after you find and correct 100 mistakes in a week.

Thousands of beautiful creatures. live and thrive under the see. amongthe many fascinating fish is one called the Red Firefish. this fish have poisonous spines on its back that protect it from othe rfish.

Another interesting fish are the Triggerfish. It has orange and purbple stripes that make it looks much larger than it really is That is what keep other fish from attacking.

Butterflyfish have dark spot on their tails that look like eyes. This is confuseing to other fish that think the head is actually where the tail should be.

The sea are full of wunderful creatures. These three fishers are no exception.

HOW WELL DO YOU USE YOUR TIME?

If you use your time well, it will seem like you have more time to get things done. Take the following survey to find out how well you use your time.

Name ____________________________________

Directions

Read each statement and circle a number from 0–4. Total your points and check your score at the bottom to see how well you organize your time.

0 = never **1 = occasionally** **2 = sometimes** **3 = often** **4 = always**

	Statement					
1	My free time doesn't get in the way of my study time.	0	1	2	3	4
2	I always do important things first.	0	1	2	3	4
3	I use a calendar to keep track of dates and deadlines.	0	1	2	3	4
4	I break large assignments into smaller steps.	0	1	2	3	4
5	I can estimate how long activities and assignments will take.	0	1	2	3	4
6	I have a special time to study every day.	0	1	2	3	4
7	I do assignments in the most efficient order.	0	1	2	3	4
8	I take breaks when I need them.	0	1	2	3	4

If you scored

- **28 or above,** *congratulations! Are you ready to get even better?*
- **20–27,** *you're doing quite well. A few timely tips and you'll have time management figured out.*
- **9–19,** *you've still got time to improve. Pay attention to upcoming lessons; they'll be worth your time.*
- **0–8,** *time is getting away from you! Get ready to learn some timely tips!*

Name ____________________

Prioritizing

A good way to manage your time is to make a prioritized "to-do" list so the most important tasks are completed first and less important ones are completed last.

Directions

Rewrite the following to-do lists so the person completes the most important tasks first and the less important ones last. When you're done, meet with two or three classmates and explain why you put each task in its place. Together, make new lists that combine your group's best ideas. To continue this activity, complete page 23.

To-Do List
1. Read "Forest Survival."
2. Sharpen antlers.
3. Eat a tree-bark lunch.

To-do lists work on weekdays, weekends, or any time you need to organize your time.

Monday After-School To-Do List	Revised List
1. Shop for Mom's birthday present.	**1.** ____________
2. Clean my room.	**2.** ____________
3. Play soccer with Jack.	**3.** ____________
4. Study for tomorrow's history test.	**4.** ____________

Tuesday Before-School To-Do List	Revised List
1. Walk the dog for fun.	**1.** ____________
2. Pack my backpack for school.	**2.** ____________
3. Double-check my homework.	**3.** ____________
4. Call Sam for a ride to school.	**4.** ____________

Saturday To-Do List	Revised List
1. Watch TV.	**1.** ____________
2. Hang around the mall.	**2.** ____________
3. Mow the lawn.	**3.** ____________
4. Work on my book report for Monday.	**4.** ____________

Name ______________________________

Directions

Make a list of "to dos" for tomorrow. List activities from the time school gets out until you go to bed. (Use ideas from the revised lists on page 22 if you can't think of anything.) Be sure you set priorities and list important tasks first.

To-Do List for Tomorrow (from school dismissal until bedtime)

1. ______________________________
2. ______________________________
3. ______________________________
4. ______________________________
5. ______________________________
6. ______________________________
7. ______________________________
8. ______________________________

Show your list to a friend. Does he or she agree that you set priorities and listed your tasks in order from most to least important? Revise your list if necessary.

Name ____________________

Track Your Time

A person who knows how he or she spends the day is more likely to manage time efficiently.

Directions

Think about what you do every day and then enter the information in the grid. (Be sure to include when you eat meals, complete homework, watch TV, have club meetings, play sports, and have free time.) To continue this activity, complete page 25.

"TRACKING YOUR TIME" GRID

	Hour	Monday	Tuesday	Wednesday	Thursday	Friday
Before School	6:00 a.m.					
	7:00 a.m.					
	8:00 a.m.					
During School	___:___ a.m. to ___:___ p.m.	S C H O O L				
After School	___:___ p.m.					
	___:___ p.m.					
	___:___ p.m.					
	___:___ p.m.					
	___:___ p.m.					
	___:___ p.m.					
	___:___ p.m.					

Name ______________________________

Directions

Review your "Tracking Your Time" Grid on page 24. Make a new grid on this page to give yourself more time for studying. Try to find at least one more hour for studying during the week. (That's only 12 minutes a day!) First copy nonchangeable activities onto the grid below. Then rearrange or delete other activities or free time.

Don't overdo it! If you find that you are constantly on the move, cut back.

"MAKING MORE TIME FOR STUDYING" GRID

	Hour	Monday	Tuesday	Wednesday	Thursday	Friday
Before School	6:00 a.m.					
	7:00 a.m.					
	8:00 a.m.					
During School	__:__ a.m. to __:__ p.m.	S	C	H	O	O L
After School	__:__ p.m.					
	__:__ p.m.					
	__:__ p.m.					
	__:__ p.m.					
	__:__ p.m.					
	__:__ p.m.					
	__:__ p.m.					

Name ______________________________

Cool Calendar

To be a good time manager, you should record information in advance so you can plan for upcoming assignments and events.

1. Write the name of a month on the top of each of 12 blank calendar pages. (You can make copies of page 27.) Put the pages in order, starting with the month in which you begin school.

2. Go through each month and write in names of important events. Include test and assignment dates, vacation dates, sports schedules, club meeting dates, birthdays, party dates, dates for music lessons . . . anything you think is important!

3. Glue each calendar page to a piece of construction paper. Use your creativity and imagination when decorating the construction-paper background for each calendar to give it a "personal touch."

4. Punch two holes in the top of each page and string them together with two loops of yarn. Attach paper clips to the yarn loops to hang your calendar.

5. Each month, add important dates to your calendar. At the end of each month, take off the paper clips and flip over the page to the next month. Then reattach the clips and hang the calendar again.

Try color-coding events for at-a-glance searching. For example, write homework in red, club dates in blue, tests in green, and so on.

Sunday	Monday	Tuesday	Wednesday	Thursday	Friday	Saturday

Name ____________________

Weekly Planner

When you know how to set priorities and make to-do lists, you can use a "weekly planner." Weekly planners are helpful for remembering all kinds of information.

Directions

Read the weekly-planner example below. Then bring the weekly-planner page on page 29 to each class and record on it all homework and important events for next week. List important tasks first.

If this is a time-management system you like, use a planner for the rest of the year. Use your school's weekly planner or place 52 blank, hole-punched weekly-planner pages in a three-ring binder or folder. Carry the planner with you to each class. Use the planner to keep track of assignments and to make to-do lists throughout the year.

Week of: November 9–13

Day	Tasks	Day	Tasks	Long-Term Assignments / Notes
M	Study for history test Study for spelling test math pp. 52–53	Th	Read science chp. 4 Study for history test Study for spelling test math pp. 59–60	**Long-Term Assignments** nonfiction book report due 11/18 (Find a book this week.)
T	Study for history test Study for spelling test math pp. 54–56	F	History test (Chapter 3) Spelling test (Unit 8)	**Notes** *Don't forget to bring nonfiction book home!
W	Study for history test Study for spelling test math pp. 57–58	Sa	Read nonfiction book	**To-Do List** Study for history Study for spelling
		S	Read nonfiction book	

Week of: ______________________________

M

Th

Long-Term Assignments

T

F

Notes

W

Sa

To-Do List

S

Name ______________________________

Homework Grid

A good way to make time for homework is to record at-home assignments on a special grid that gives you a chance to see homework all by itself.

Directions

Complete the grid to record tonight's homework assignments. Write a number in the last column to show the order in which you will complete the work. Then make copies of the grid on page 31 and use them throughout the year.

If this is a time-management system you like, use one grid each week. Bring a grid to class every day, record assignments, and bring the grid home every night.

HOMEWORK GRID

Subject	Assignment	Due Date	Priority

HOMEWORK GRID

Subject	Assignment	Due Date	Priority

Name ______________________

Step by Step

It helps to break down a big assignment into smaller parts to make time for each part. Then, the assignment won't seem so overwhelming.

Directions

Read the example below to see how easy it can be to break up a big assignment. Then complete the activity on page 33.

Assignment

Book report for a 240-page book that has not yet been read. Due in two weeks (14 days).

Step 1

List the "big jobs" necessary to complete the assignment. Write them in the order in which they should be done.

1. Read the book.

2. Prepare the report.

Record the steps for completing a big assignment on a calendar so you don't forget to do them.

Step 2

Divide the number of days you have to complete the assignment by the number of big jobs. Your answer will be the number of days you have to complete each big job. *14 days ÷ 2 big jobs = 7 days for each big job*

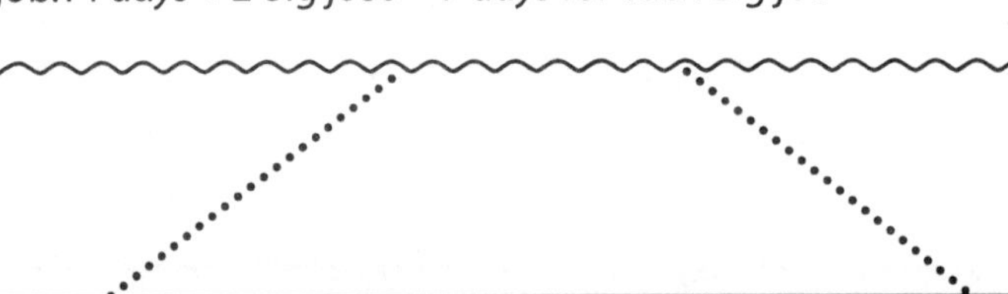

Step 3

Divide the big jobs into smaller parts so you can complete one small part each day.

I have 7 days to read the book. (The book is 240 pages long.)

Day 1: 30 pages
Day 2: 35 pages
Day 3: 35 pages
Day 4: 35 pages
Day 5: 35 pages
Day 6: 35 pages
Day 7: 35 pages

I have 7 days to write and prepare the report.

Day 1: Brainstorm
Day 2: Rough Draft
Day 3: Self-Edit
Day 4: Rewrite
Day 5: Mom Edits
Day 6: Final Draft
Day 7: Illustration and Cover

Name ______________________________

Directions

Review page 32. Then read the assignment below to design your own step-by-step time schedule that divides the assignment into smaller steps.

ASSIGNMENT

Science Fair experiment and tri-fold exhibit board. Due in 14 days.

Step 1: Record Big Jobs

(List two big jobs. Not all assignments have two big jobs; some have more.)

1. ______________________________
2. ______________________________

Step 2: Calculate Number of Days to Complete Big Jobs

14 days ÷ ____ big jobs = _____ days to complete each big job

Step 3: Divide Jobs into Smaller Parts

I have _______ days to ______________________________.

Day 1: ____________________ Day 5: ____________________

Day 2: ____________________ Day 6: ____________________

Day 3: ____________________ Day 7: ____________________

Day 4: ____________________

I have _______ days to ______________________________.

Day 1: ____________________ Day 5: ____________________

Day 2: ____________________ Day 6: ____________________

Day 3: ____________________ Day 7: ____________________

Day 4: ____________________

Name ______________________

Time Judge

When you can estimate the time it takes to complete a job, you can make good choices about when to start. A good "time manager" is a good "time judge."

Directions

Estimate how long it takes you to do the following tasks. Then do them and time yourself to see how close your estimates are.

Before you begin an assignment, estimate how long it will take to complete, and divide the work if necessary.

Task	Estimated Time	Actual Time
1 Look up three vocabulary words and write their meanings.	______	______
2 Write one paragraph about what you did last night.	______	______
3 Cut three headlines from the newspaper.	______	______
4 Complete five long division problems.	______	______
5 Read two pages in a fiction book.	______	______
6 Read two pages in a social studies book and take notes on it.	______	______
7 Copy your spelling words five times.	______	______
8 Make your lunch.	______	______
9 Do 20 sit-ups.	______	______
10 Write the alphabet in your best cursive handwriting.	______	______

Name ____________________

Time-Savers

When you complete schoolwork in a logical order, it gets done much faster!

Directions

Think about the following homework assignment. How would you complete it to do a good job and save time? Write each step for completing the assignment and the amount of time you think each step would take. Add up the time. Compare your steps and times with a partner's to see who is the better "time-saver."

ASSIGNMENT

Design a poster about saving the manatee (sea cow). Include at least five facts about manatees and list the name and phone number of at least one organization that tries to help them. Paint or color your poster.

How I Would Complete the Assignment	Estimated Time
STEP 1 ____________________	________
STEP 2 ____________________	________
STEP 3 ____________________	________
STEP 4 ____________________	________
STEP 5 ____________________	________
STEP 6 ____________________	________

Total Time ________

One great time-saver is to have all your materials ready before you begin an assignment.

Name ____________________

Taking Breaks

If you can't concentrate when studying, or you become bored, frustrated, or tired, take a break. A little time off can get you back on track and ready to learn.

Directions

Think back to past study sessions or projects. When did you need a break? Write your ideas on the lines below. Then read the kinds of breaks you might like, circle the ones that appeal to you, and write in your own ideas.

Don't take a long break that "eats up" all your study time. And if you're "on a roll" and don't feel like you need a break, keep going!

Times When I Need a Break

Example: I need a break after I read for a half hour.

1. ____________________
2. ____________________
3. ____________________
4. ____________________
5. ____________________

Breaks I Might Like

(Circle one or more. You can write in your own ideas.)

1. Snack Break
2. Walk or Ride My Bike
3. Phone Call to a Friend
4. Music Break
5. Computer Game
6. ____________________
7. ____________________
8. ____________________
9. ____________________
10. ____________________

CAN YOU FIND & REMEMBER INFORMATION WHEN YOU'RE READING?

Do you use strategies that help you remember what you read? Take the following survey to find out.

Name ______________________________

Directions

Read each statement and circle a number from 0–4. (If you don't know about the strategy, mark 0.) Total your points and check your score at the bottom to see how well you can find and remember information when you read.

0 = never **1 = occasionally** **2 = sometimes** **3 = often** **4 = always**

1	Before I read a chapter or book, I know what my teacher wants me to learn from it.	0	1	2	3	4
2	I know how to preview reading material to get the most information from it.	0	1	2	3	4
3	I can read a paragraph and pick out the main idea and important details.	0	1	2	3	4
4	I can read a textbook chapter and answer all the questions at the end of the chapter without a problem.	0	1	2	3	4
5	I know how to use the SQ3R method.	0	1	2	3	4
6	I know how to skim reading material to get the main idea.	0	1	2	3	4
7	I know how to scan reading material to find answers to questions.	0	1	2	3	4
8	I make "pictures in my head" when I'm reading.	0	1	2	3	4

If you scored

- **28 or above,** *congratulations! Now you get to learn a few new tips to make things easier.*
- **19–27,** *good job. With a few tips, you'll be remembering a lot more.*
- **10–18,** *you need some help finding and remembering information. Get ready for some good advice.*
- **0–9,** *it's time to change your reading habits! Get ready to learn some great tips!*

Name ______________________________

Preparing to Read

A good reader acts like a detective who previews the reading and looks for clues in a book or chapter before reading the words.

Directions

Read the following "preparing to read" tips. Circle the letter under *Good Clue* if a tip is a good idea. Circle the letter under *Get a Clue!* if the tip is a bad idea. Then write the circled letters (in order) to complete the message.

Preparing to Read Tip	Good Clue	Get a Clue!
1 Read the book/chapter title and think about it.	D	B
2 Review the book/chapter when you are really tired.	O	E
3 Read the author's name and think how this book may be like other books you've read by him or her.	T	A
4 Read the inside and outside of the book jacket and think about the information.	E	S
5 Always review the book/chapter on an empty stomach.	R	C
6 Look at all the pictures on the cover and inside the book/chapter and try to predict what it is about.	T	N
7 Look at the book/chapter under dim light.	L	I
8 Study the book/chapter and notice how it is organized, including titles, length, and section headings.	V	M
9 Read each page number 15 times before reading the book/chapter.	Y	E

Message:

Are you a good __ __ __ __ __ __ __ __ __?

Preview before you read anything—even magazine articles. You'll get more from your reading.

Name ______________________

Reading a Paragraph

Most paragraphs have a sentence or two that tells the main idea.
Try to figure out the main idea of a paragraph first and then think about the details.

Directions

Read the following paragraphs. On the lines provided, write the main idea for each paragraph.

Remember the Maine

When Christopher Columbus landed in America, he claimed it for the country of Spain. Other discoveries in the New World were also claimed for Spain. This nation soon "owned" much of the New World and became a powerful country.

If you have trouble picking out main ideas, reread the paragraph aloud or reread the first and last sentences.

The island of Cuba was one place in the New World that belonged to Spain. In the late 1800s, the people in Cuba wanted to become an independent, free country. The people of the United States understood how the Cubans felt and wanted to help Cuba become an independent nation.

In an effort to show support, the United States government sent a battleship called the *Maine* on a peacekeeping mission to Cuba. The ship's mission was to block the harbor in an effort to protect the lives and property of the Cuban people in case of riot.

On February 15, 1898, only 25 days after its arrival, the *Maine* was destroyed by an underwater explosion. Spain was believed to be responsible. About 260 crew members were killed. The people of the United States were furious with the Spanish government and were prepared to go to war with Spain. With the battle cry, *Remember the Maine!*, the United States declared war on Spain on April 25, 1898, to help free Cuba.

Main Idea for Paragraph One ______________________

____

Main Idea for Paragraph Two ______________________

____

Main Idea for Paragraph Three ______________________

____

Main Idea for Paragraph Four ______________________

____

Name ______________________

Reading a Textbook Chapter

To become a better reader, learn how to review and read a textbook chapter so you can get the most information possible.

Directions

Meet with a group of classmates and read the pyramid. Use the words in the word bank to fill the blank(s) in each sentence. Then be ready to use the Reading Pyramid for the activity on page 41.

Reading Pyramid

Always read in a well-lit room!

1. Read the t______________ of the chapter.

2. R______________ any pictures in the chapter. Brainstorm and write down questions about the p______________.

3. Read any **boldface** words t______________ the chapter. Brainstorm and write down q______________ about the words.

4. Read the questions at the end of the chapter. Pick out k______________ words from the questions and write them down.

5. Read the opening paragraph at the b______________ of the chapter and the s______________ at the end (if there is one). Ask yourself, *What will this chapter be about?*

6. Read the chapter c______________ once without interruption. Try to answer all the questions you wrote down. Review the key words you wrote and be sure you understand their m______________. Go back and read the chapter a______________ to answer any questions you couldn't and to find any key words you m______________.

WORD BANK

key meaning beginning title carefully again
throughout review pictures summary missed questions

Name ________________________________

Directions

Choose a chapter from one of your current textbooks. Use the Reading Pyramid on page 40 as a guide to complete the following grid about your chapter.

Pyramid Grid

1. Chapter Title

____

2. Review pictures. Write questions about pictures.

____

____

____

____

3. Review boldface words. Write questions about the words.

____

____

____

____

____

4. Read questions at the end. Write key words from the questions.

____

____

5. Read the opening paragraph and the summary. Write an answer to the question *What will this chapter be about?*

____

____

6. Read the chapter once. Can you answer all your questions? Did you find the key words? Was your prediction correct? Read the chapter again to answer anything you missed the first time.

Name ______________________________

Scanning

A good reader knows how to read and then scan for answers to questions. A good scanner is usually a good test-taker! Are you a good scanner?

How to Scan

1. Before you begin, read the questions at the end of the passage or chapter. What are they asking you to find? A date? A place? A name? A reason why something happened?

2. Carefully read the passage to understand all the ideas.

3. After you read the passage, read the first question again. To find the answer, put your pointer finger on the first word of the passage or chapter and move your finger slowly down the page. Be sure your eyes follow your finger and look at the words.

4. Look for the answer to each question as you read.

5. When you find an answer, write it down in a complete sentence.

6. Go to the second question, think about it, and scan for the answer. Continue with the other questions, scanning for one answer at a time.

Directions

Follow the directions on the left to scan the passage on page 43 titled *The Early Life of George Washington Carver* and answer questions about it. Then use scanning in real life whenever you have to answer questions about something you read.

Scanning is especially helpful when you take reading tests!

Name ______________________________

Directions

Follow the directions on page 42 to scan for the answer to the question at the end of the passage. Then answer the survey questions below.

The Early Life of George Washington Carver

George Washington Carver, the brilliant African-American scientist, was born the son of a slave sometime between the years of 1858 and 1860. In 1864, slave robbers stole George and his mother from Moses Carver's farm in Missouri. George was found and returned to Moses Carver, but his mother did not return. After that, Moses Carver and his wife cared for George and his brother. During his boyhood years with the Carvers, George learned to study and care for plants. To all the neighbors, he became known as the "Plant Doctor."

Question: In what state did George Washington Carver live as a boy?

Survey Questions

1. What was the answer to the question?

____
____
____
____

2. Was scanning for the answer quicker than rereading the whole paragraph?____________________Why?

____
____
____
____

3. In which real-life situations would scanning be beneficial for you?

____
____
____
____

Name ______________________________

Skimming

A good reader knows how to skim a paragraph or chapter to find main ideas and understand what the text is about.

Directions

Follow the directions on the right to skim the passage on page 45 titled *The Early Life of Albert Einstein* and answer questions about it. Then use skimming in real life when you have to quickly understand the main idea.

How to Skim

1. Carefully read the title and first sentence of the passage/chapter, using your pointer finger as a highlighter. What do you think the passage/chapter will be about? Think about it.

2. Zigzag your finger from left to right down the passage/chapter. As you zigzag, read only important words, such as nouns and verbs. Ignore "little words," such as *the, and,* and *of.* Stop at the beginning of the last sentence of the first paragraph.

3. Carefully read the last sentence.

4. If you are reading a chapter, continue skimming each paragraph until the chapter is complete.

Skimming is especially helpful when you need a quick review or when you need to search for the main idea.

Name ______________________________

Directions

Follow the directions on page 44 to skim for the main idea in the following paragraph. Then answer the survey questions below.

The Early Life of Albert Einstein

Albert Einstein, the brilliant German scientist, was born on March 14, 1879, in the city of Ulm, Germany. He and his family moved to Munich before Albert was a year old. As a schoolboy, Albert did well in mathematics, but poorly in the rest of his subjects. He showed great intelligence, but disliked studying things that did not interest him. School became even more difficult for Albert after his family moved, without him, to Milan, Italy. Who knew that Albert would someday become the physicist who conceived the Theory of Relativity (the theory that led to the development of atomic energy)?

Survey Questions

1. What was the main idea of the paragraph?

____

____

2. Which important words "stood out" as you were skimming?

____

____

____

____

3. In what situations would skimming be beneficial for you?

____

____

____

____

____

____

____

____

Name ____________________

SQ3R

SQ3R is a great technique for remembering what you read in an assignment. If you use SQ3R when you read, you're sure to get a lot more from your study time.

Directions

Choose a textbook reading assignment. Write on a piece of notebook paper and follow the five steps below. Then use SQ3R for future assignments to be sure to get the most from your reading.

Example:

Survey
Chapter Title: The Kon-Tiki
Headings: The Raft, Why They Sailed, A Successful Trip
Words: Polynesians, Thor Heyerdahl, Stone Age

Question
a. Could Stone Age Europeans have sailed around the world in rafts?
b. Did Thor and his crew prove it?
c. If they did, how long did it take?

Review
a. They could have, which would explain a group of light-skinned Polynesians.
b. Yes. They sailed in a raft from Peru to the Polynesian Islands.
c. It took 97 days.

1 Survey

Take a general survey of the pages before you begin reading. Look at the chapter headings, special vocabulary, introductory and summary paragraphs, and any diagrams and pictures.
(To show you completed this step, write down the chapter title, headings, and special vocabulary words on your paper.)

2 Question

Think about what you surveyed and write down several questions you think will be answered in the reading.
(Write your questions.)

3 Read

Read the assignment to find the answers to your questions.

4 Recite

When you find the answers, recite them aloud.

5 Review

After reading and reciting, review what you have read.
(To review, jot down answers to the questions and other important information you think you need to remember.)

SQ3R is especially helpful for social studies and science reading or when you need to take notes for research papers.

Name ______________________

Reading Novels

A graphic organizer is a great way to record and remember information from a novel.

Directions

Think about a novel you are currently reading. Record information from the novel on the graphic organizer to show what you need to remember from this book. Save and use the graphic organizer on page 48 for a different novel.

Characters

Setting(s)

Main Idea

Title

____

____

Author

____

Resolution

Ending

Problem

Climax

STUDY BUDDY TIP

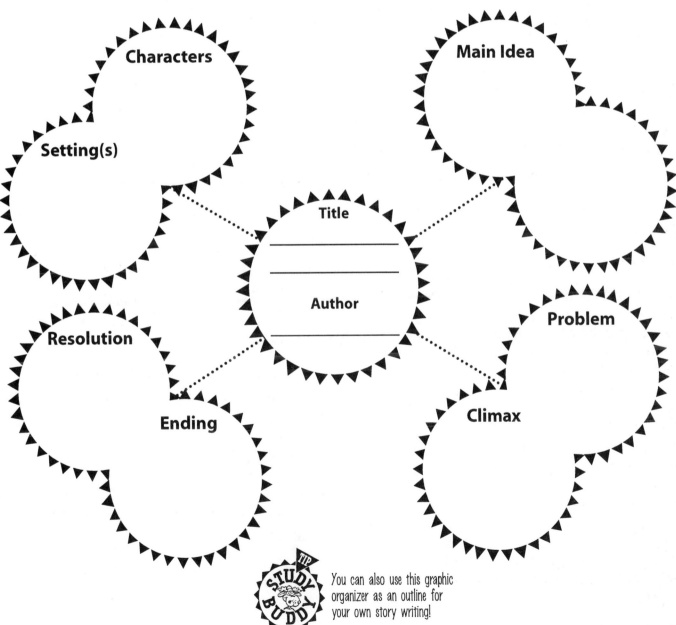

You can also use this graphic organizer as an outline for your own story writing!

Name ______________________________

Directions

Review your work on page 47, and use the following graphic organizer to record and remember information from a novel.

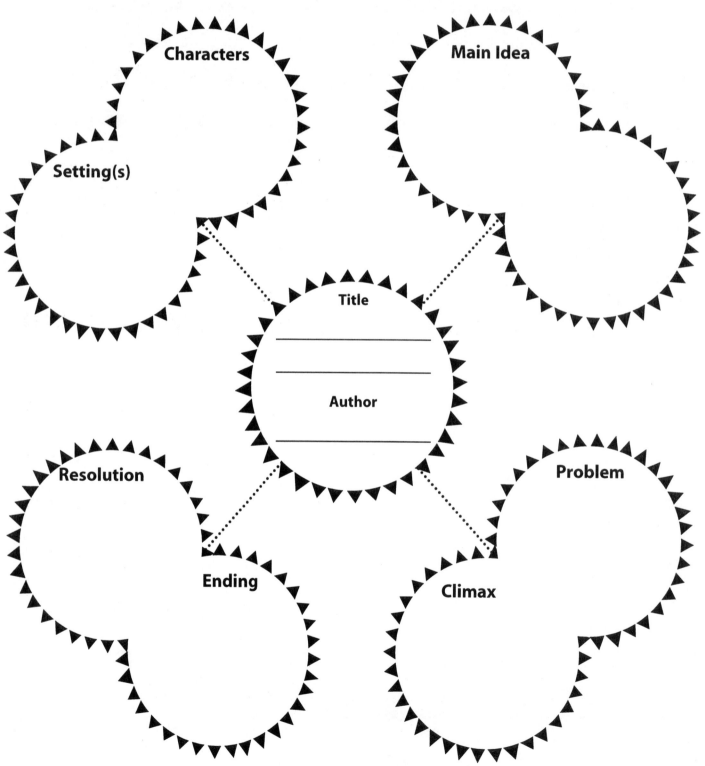

Characters

Main Idea

Setting(s)

Title

____

____

Author

____

Resolution

Problem

Ending

Climax

ARE YOU A GOOD NOTE-TAKER?

Taking good notes can really improve your study techniques and increase your knowledge. Do you take good notes? Take the following survey to find out.

Name ______________________________

Directions

Read each statement and circle a number from 0–4. Total your points and check your score at the bottom to see how well you take notes.

0 = never **1 = occasionally** **2 = sometimes** **3 = often** **4 = always**

	Statement					
1	I take notes as I read.	0	1	2	3	4
2	I take notes as I listen to a speaker.	0	1	2	3	4
3	I use symbols and shorten words in my notes to record information more quickly.	0	1	2	3	4
4	I ask questions in class.	0	1	2	3	4
5	I create good outlines from my notes.	0	1	2	3	4

If you scored

- **17 or above,** *congratulations! That's a noteworthy accomplishment! Now get ready for more great ideas.*
- **13–16,** *nice job. The upcoming note-taking tips will have you in the top category in no time!*
- **9–12,** *your notes need more notice from you. Have your pencil ready for some note-taking advice.*
- **0–8,** *take note and pay attention to the upcoming note-taking suggestions.*

Name ______________________

Taking Notes as You Read

Knowing how to take notes as you read helps you remember information and use it to study for tests or to complete homework.

Directions

Read the article on page 51 and follow the directions below to take notes on it. Practice taking notes this way whenever you read a textbook.

1. Fold a piece of lined notebook paper in half lengthwise. Write the title of the article/chapter and the page numbers at the top of the paper.
2. Review all pictures and questions that appear in the article/chapter.
3. Read the opening paragraph and write a one-sentence summary across the top of the entire paper.
4. Write the first boldface heading on the left side of the paper. Read the paragraph under the heading. Write any key words from the paragraph on the right side of the paper, directly across from the heading. (If there is more than one paragraph under a heading, write key words from all the paragraphs.) Repeat this step for each heading and paragraph.
5. Read the closing paragraph and write a one-sentence summary across the bottom of the entire paper.
6. Reread the questions from the article/chapter. Skim your notes to see if you answered them. If you cannot find the answers in your notes, scan the article to find the answers and add them to your notes.
7. To review and study for a test, read the boldface headings out loud several times and then the corresponding information to the right. Then fold your paper in half. Read the boldface headings only and try to remember the information to the right. Practice until you can remember all the information.

Example:

Fishy Facts	p.17
Fish breathe through	gills.
Gills	* little openings
	* both sides of head
	* H_2O goes in mouth and
	out gills
	* draw oxygen from H_2O as
	they transfer it from mouth to
	gills
All animals, including	fish, need oxygen to
survive.	

Don't forget to save your notes in a folder or binder so you can use them to study for a test.

Name ______________________________

Directions

Read the following article and complete the note-taking directions on page 50.

Gila Monsters

Gila monster is the common name for the largest lizard in the United States. Gila monsters can be found in the deserts of Arizona, Utah, New Mexico, and northwestern Mexico.

Physical Characteristics

Gila monsters have a stocky build and four short, slow-moving legs. They have thick, blunt tails in which fat is stored. This fat allows a Gila monster to live for months without food. An adult Gila monster can grow up to two feet long. Gila monsters are often black with pink, orange, yellow, or white bumpy "beads" on their bodies. They have a flat, forked tongue.

Protective Adaptation

The Gila monster is one of only two poisonous lizards in the world. (The other is the beaded lizard, found in Mexico and Guatemala.) A Gila monster secretes poison through glands in its lower jaw. When a Gila monster bites, the poison flows out of the glands and along grooves on its teeth. Although their bites are harmful to humans, Gila monsters rarely bite people.

Eating Habits

Gila monsters generally eat rodents, young birds, and eggs. To eat eggs, they break them and lick up the liquid inside. Live prey is eaten whole.

Reproduction

Like all reptiles, Gila monsters lay eggs. Their eggs are leathery and about the size of chicken eggs. Female Gila monsters lay about a dozen eggs in a sandy hole, cover them, and then abandon them. The babies hatch in about a month.

Write the answers to these questions at the bottom of your notes if the answers aren't in your notes.

Question 1: How long can Gila monsters grow?

Question 2: Are Gila monsters poisonous?

Question 3: What do Gila monsters eat?

Question 4: Where do Gila monsters lay their eggs?

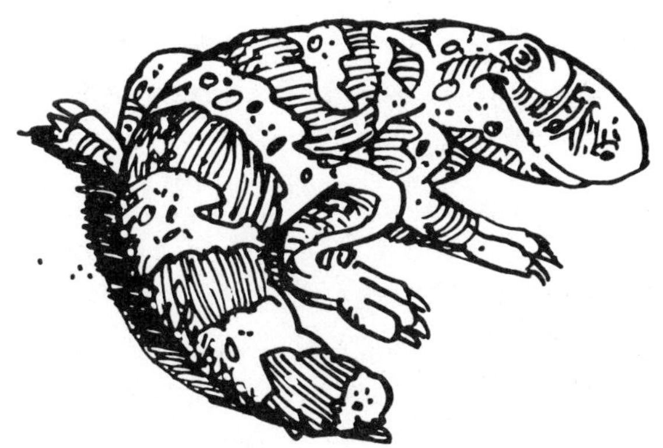

Name ______________________________

Taking Notes as You Listen

Taking notes as you listen requires practice, concentration, and good listening skills.

Directions

Have a partner choose a paragraph from page 53 and slowly read it aloud to you. Follow the note-taking directions on the right as your partner reads. Then trade places and read the other paragraph so your partner can take notes.

1. Look at the speaker and concentrate on what he or she is saying.
2. Write down key words and phrases only; no full sentences.
3. Abbreviate words so you can write more quickly.
4. Skip lines between each idea so you can add more information later.
5. Pay attention when the speaker raises his or her voice or makes gestures; write down the accompanying information.

Write Your Notes Here

____

____

____

____

____

____

____

____

____

____

____

____

____

____

____

When you take notes in class, ask questions if you missed any information. Listen for hints such as *You will need to remember this, This is really important, Be sure to write this down, Spell that correctly, Let me go over this again, Let's review,* or *This isn't in the book, but you should remember it.* Copy any diagrams, words, or definitions written on the board.

Name ____________________

Directions

Carefully read aloud to a partner one of the following paragraphs and have him or her take notes on page 52. Then trade places and have your partner read the other paragraph as you take notes.

The Early Life of John F. Kennedy

John Fitzgerald Kennedy, the 35th President of the United States, was born on May 29, 1917, in Massachusetts. John was the second of nine children born to Joseph Kennedy, a multi-millionaire businessman, and Rose Kennedy, the daughter of a former mayor of Boston. As a young boy, John was thin and sickly. When it was time to begin school, John attended a boarding school called Choate, where he was very popular and had many friends. During the summers, John and his family lived at a home in Hyannis Port, Massachusetts. John had his own sailboat and was an excellent swimmer and sailor. After high school, John attended Harvard University and played football his freshman year. After a football-related back injury, John took some time off school to travel in Europe. He soon returned to Harvard, where he excelled in his studies and even wrote a best-selling book.

The Early Life of Abraham Lincoln

Abraham Lincoln, the 16th President of the United States, was born on February 12, 1809. Abe was the second child born to Thomas and Nancy Hanks Lincoln, pioneers who farmed and lived in a one-room log cabin in western Kentucky. Abe and his older sister, Sally, worked on the farm and went to school when they had the time. They attended a one-room schoolhouse, which was called a "blab" school because the students recited their lessons aloud together. By the time Abe was six, he could read and write. When he was seven, Abe's family moved to the Indiana territory. In 1818, Abe's mother passed away, leaving the family sad and lonely. A year later, Thomas Lincoln married a widow, Sarah Bush Lincoln, who brought three children to the family. When Abe was 19, he got a job on a flatboat carrying meat and crops along the Ohio and Mississippi rivers. By 1830, Abe and his family moved to Illinois, where Abe owned a store, husked corn, split logs, repaired houses, and wrote letters and deeds.

Name ______________________________

Note-Taking Short Cuts

You can use "short cuts" when taking notes to shorten words and write important information as quickly as possible.

Directions

Read the following short-cut list below. Then read the words without symbols and write a list of your own short cuts. Keep this list with you and incorporate the short cuts when you take notes.

Don't overuse short cuts. If you do, you may not be able to understand what you wrote.

Word	Symbol	Word	Symbol
at	@	social studies	SS
money	$	science	Sc.
number	#	language arts	LA
and	&	math	M
important	*	north	N
plus	+	south	S
minus	-	east	E
multiply	x	west	W
divide	÷	with	w/
equal to	=	without	w/o
not equal to	≠	because	
similar to	≈	in the morning	
less than	<	in the afternoon	
greater than	>	memorize	
question	?	on the test	
check	√	read	
paragraph	¶	reread	
page	p.	homework	
pages	pp.	degrees	
chapter	ch.	half	
yes	y	percent	
no	n	approximately	
example	e.g.	definition	

Name ______________________________

Asking Questions for Better Notes

When you ask questions, you gain information and show the teacher that you really want to learn.

Directions

Circle *T* for each true statement and *F* for each false one. Meet with a partner to check your answers. Then discuss the statements as a class and get your teacher's point of view.

1. You should wait for someone else to ask a question so you don't sound stupid. **T** **F**
2. When doing homework, you should write down questions to ask the next day. **T** **F**
3. You should shout out questions without raising your hand. **T** **F**
4. You should get all your questions answered, even if it means staying after school (when you can). **T** **F**
5. You should listen carefully to the answer given and write down the answer so you won't forget. **T** **F**
6. You should politely ask the teacher to explain the answer again if you did not understand the answer the first time. **T** **F**
7. You should ask questions you already know the answers to and take up class time. **T** **F**

If you're shy, ask the teacher if you can meet privately with him or her a few times a week to get questions answered.

Name ______________________________

Creating an Outline from Your Notes

At times it's good to use an outline to create an organized, easy-to-follow study guide. Outlines are also used for organizing ideas for reports and speeches.

TITLE

I. Main Topic One (a "big idea" and broad topic)

A. Subtopic related to main topic *(an idea related to the big idea)*

1. Detail related to subtopic (a detail about the smaller idea)
2. Detail related to subtopic (a detail about the smaller idea)

B. Subtopic

1. Detail
2. Detail

II. Main Topic Two

A. Subtopic

1. Detail
2. Detail

B. Subtopic

1. Detail
2. Detail

III. Main Topic Three

A. Subtopic

1. Detail
2. Detail

B. Subtopic

1. Detail
2. Detail

Directions

Read the following outline format and notice how an outline is organized. Then read the word boxes on page 57. Cut out the words and glue them in the correct places on page 58 to form a real outline.

Social studies notes make excellent outlines!

Name ______________________

Directions

Read the words under the headings on the following grid. Cut out the word boxes and glue them in the correct places on page 58 to form a real outline.

OUTLINE INFORMATION FOR TYRANNOSAURUS REX

Information for Main Topic One: BODY
Body Adaptations
3-foot (90-cm) jaws with 60 sharp teeth
2 long, strong, clawed legs and 2 short arms
Up to 18 feet (5.6 m) high
Size
Up to 50 feet (15 m) long

Information for Main Topic Two: REPRODUCTION
Nests
Holes the size of the diameter of the mother's body
Up to 15 eggs in one grouping
Eggs
Eggs were proportionately smaller in size compared to bird eggs
Crater-like holes dug next to streams

Information for Main Topic Three: HABITAT
Fewer plant and animal species
Regions
Western North America
Warmer temperatures than today
Environmental Conditions
Mongolia

Name ______________________________

Directions

Cut out the word boxes from page 57 and glue them in the correct places on the following outline.

Title: Tyrannosaurus Rex

I. BODY

A. [ ]

1. [ ]
2. [ ]

B. [ ]

1. [ ]
2. [ ]

II. REPRODUCTION

A. [ ]

1. [ ]
2. [ ]

B. [ ]

1. [ ]
2. [ ]

III. HABITAT

A. [ ]

1. [ ]
2. [ ]

B. [ ]

1. [ ]
2. [ ]

Name ______________________________

Writing Your Own Outline

It takes practice to write a good outline. But once you know how to write one, you can organize a lot of information in just a little time.

Directions

Read a paragraph from a page in a textbook or one that your teacher assigns you. Meet with a partner to write an outline that records information from the paragraph. (You don't have to fill up all the lines, but they are there if you need them.) There is only one main topic because a single paragraph usually has one main idea.

Title: ______________________________

I. ______________________________

A. ______________________________

1. ______________________________
2. ______________________________
3. ______________________________
4. ______________________________
5. ______________________________

B. ______________________________

1. ______________________________
2. ______________________________
3. ______________________________
4. ______________________________
5. ______________________________

C. ______________________________

1. ______________________________
2. ______________________________
3. ______________________________
4. ______________________________
5. ______________________________

Outlines make terrific study guides for tests.

Name ______________________

Using Your Notes

You should always study your notes to learn the information in them. You can make the most of your note-studying time by trying some of the following tips.

Directions

Choose one page of notes that you have taken recently. Use the tips in the left column to commit the information from your notes to memory. Follow the directions in the middle column to test yourself and see if you learned from your notes. Then write answers to the questions in the right column.

	Tip	Test	Question
1	Find five key words in your notes. Read each word aloud ten times.	Without looking at your notes, say each key word.	Did you remember all the key words? ______________
2	Choose three important facts from your notes. Write each fact four times in a row. Read aloud what you wrote.	Without looking at your notes, write each fact.	Could you remember all the facts? ______________
3	What was the main idea in your notes? In your own words, tell the main idea to three friends or family members. Tell them why you think your answer is correct.	Have your friends or family members read your notes. Ask each person to explain why he or she thinks your answer was correct or incorrect.	Did you really know the main idea in your notes? ______________

Try these techniques whenever you study from your notes. You will remember the information in no time!

HOW WELL DO YOU GIVE AN ORAL PRESENTATION?

Oral presentations can be fun when you know how to give them. Take this survey to find out how well you handle oral presentations.

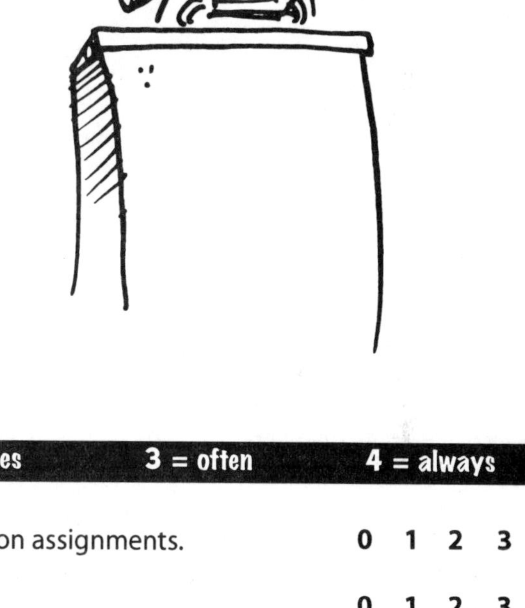

Name ______________________________

Directions

Read each statement and circle a number from 0–4. Total your points and check your score at the bottom to see how well you give oral presentations.

0 = never   1 = occasionally   2 = sometimes   3 = often   4 = always

	Statement					
1	I know the kinds of questions to ask about oral-presentation assignments.	0	1	2	3	4
2	I know how to make an outline for an oral presentation.	0	1	2	3	4
3	I can prepare note cards for an oral presentation.	0	1	2	3	4
4	I know how to practice oral presentations so they're easy to give.	0	1	2	3	4
5	I can use books and computers to find facts to support oral presentations.	0	1	2	3	4
6	I know how to make my oral presentations really interesting.	0	1	2	3	4
7	I know about and use "public speaking" techniques.	0	1	2	3	4

If you scored

- **22 or above,** *way to go! Get ready for some ideas to help you make your presentations even better!*
- **15–21,** *good job. Incorporate a few of the upcoming techniques and you'll soon be a professional speaker.*
- **8–14,** *you need a little help. Pay close attention to the oral presentation activities!*
- **0–7,** *get ready. The upcoming techniques deserve your attention!*

Name ____________________

Getting the Facts

You should ask plenty of questions in class to get as much information as possible about an oral presentation before you begin the assignment.

Directions

Read the oral-presentation description and answer the questions that follow on this page and page 63. Keep these questions so you can ask the same questions when you're assigned a real oral presentation.

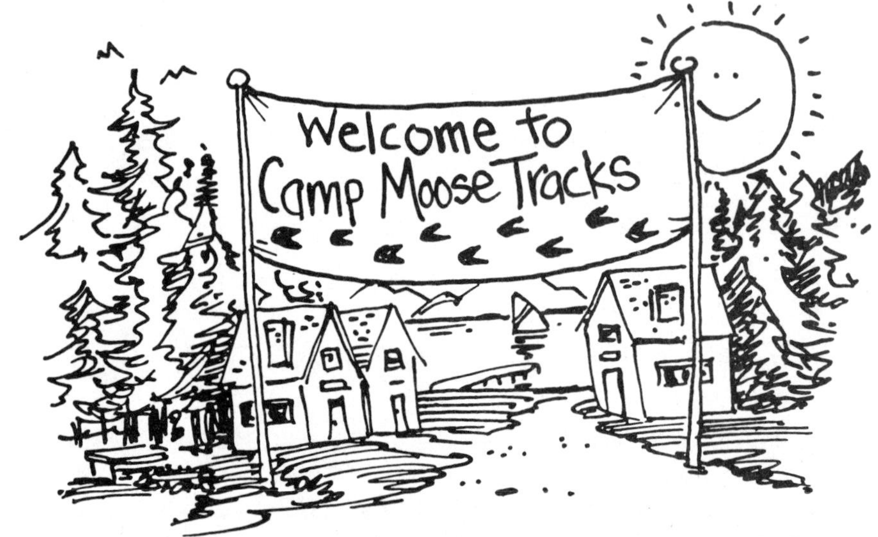

Oral-Presentation Description for English Class

You have been assigned to give a narrative oral presentation about your favorite summer memory. You are to speak one week from today's date. The speech should be at least four minutes long. The speech should be recorded on note cards. You should provide at least one photograph or illustration. You can use the chalkboard to draw visual aids. You should show and describe at least one memento as a prop. Since the speech is about you, there is no need for a bibliography.

1. In which class has the speech been assigned? ____________________

2. What is the subject of the speech? ____________________

3. When will you give the speech? ____________________

4. What kind of speech is it?

   a. demonstration

   b. persuasive

   c. informational

   d. narrative

If the class won't be your audience, find out to whom you'll be speaking so you can prepare the speech to meet their needs.

Name ____________________

5 How many minutes do you have to speak?____________________

6 How will you record your speech?

a. outline

b. note cards

c. written word for word

7 Do you have to provide photographs, illustrations, or charts?

a. yes

b. no

8 What kind of visual/auditory aids can you use?

a. overhead projector

b. computer projection

c. cassette-tape recording

d. chalkboard

e. videotape

f. chart paper

9 Are props required?

a. yes

b. no

10 If the speech has to have a bibliography, how many sources are needed?

____

Name ________________________________

Outline for a Speech

It's a good idea to make an outline for a speech before transferring information to note cards.

Directions

Use the following format to make an outline for a demonstration speech about how to make a pitcher of iced tea. (You don't have to fill up all the lines, but they are there in case you need them.)

It's a good idea to use props when you give a demonstration speech.

I. Gather all the ingredients and utensils. Show and tell about all the ingredients and where you got them.

A. ________________________________

B. ________________________________

C. ________________________________

D. ________________________________

E. ________________________________

II. Make the tea. Show and tell the order in which the tea is made. Explain each detail, including which utensils you use and how you use them.

A. ________________________________

B. ________________________________

C. ________________________________

D. ________________________________

E. ________________________________

F. ________________________________

G. ________________________________

III. Clean up and put away all the ingredients and utensils before taking a sip. Show and tell how to clean up.

A. ________________________________

B. ________________________________

C. ________________________________

D. ________________________________

E. ________________________________

Name ______________________________

Preparing an Oral Presentation

If you're a good public speaker, you have prepared and practiced for your speech—so getting up in front of the class is no big deal!

Directions

Read the steps for giving an oral presentation. Then look at the pictures that describe the steps. Draw a line from each step to its picture.

a.

b.

c.

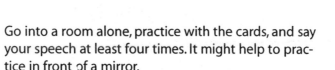

1. Transfer short phrases from your outline to note cards. (Write one main idea per note card.)
2. Lay out the cards in front of you. Place them in a logical order and number them.
3. Pick and choose. Do you want to include all the information? Should you eliminate any cards? Should you add any cards?
4. Place the cards in order again. Think of an exciting opening and a strong ending. Write each idea on a note card and place the cards at the top and bottom of the card pile. If required, gather props.
5. Go into a room alone, practice with the cards, and say your speech at least four times. It might help to practice in front of a mirror.
6. Practice your speech in front of your family or friends at least once.
7. Just before the speech, silently review your cards and picture your speech in your head.
8. When you give the speech, speak loudly and clearly, look at the audience, smile, and be natural.

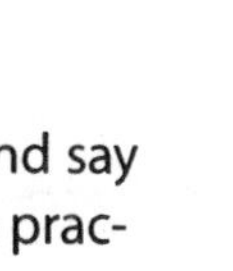

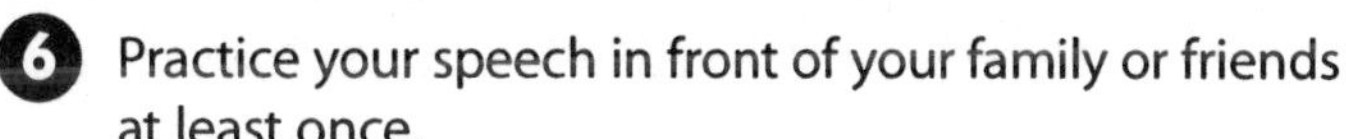

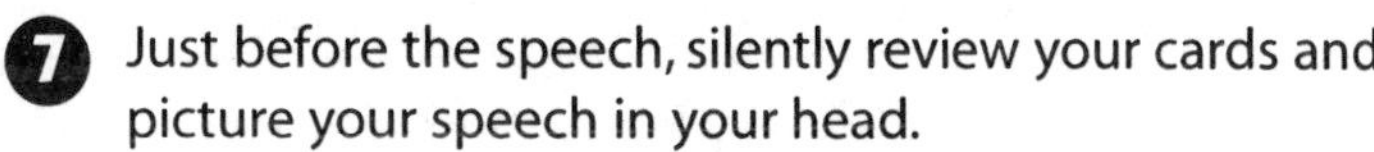

e.

d.

f.

h.

g.

It's best not to memorize a speech word for word. If you do, you might speak too quickly or forget the words.

Name ____________________

Public-Speaking Tips

With a little practice, even the shyest person can give a great oral presentation. Try the following activity to learn some terrific public-speaking skills.

Directions

Read the public-speaking tips on this page and page 67. Write *yes* next to the tip if you should follow it and *no* if you should not follow it. Then explain each answer. After you have finished, meet with a group of friends and talk about the answers. As a group, design a poster that gives public-speaking tips based on your group's best answers.

1. Give a speech without practicing it first. ____________
   Explain your answer. ____________________
   ____
   ____

2. Place your note cards in order before you give your speech. ____________
   Explain your answer. ____________________
   ____
   ____

3. During your speech, leave your props at your desk and run back and forth to get them. ____________
   Explain your answer. ____________________
   ____
   ____

4. Say each word clearly and loudly. ____________
   Explain your answer. ____________________
   ____
   ____

5. Turn your back to the audience. ____________
   Explain your answer. ____________________
   ____
   ____

Name ____________________________

6. Speak with expression to make your points. __________
Explain your answer. ____
____
____

7. Look down at your note cards the whole time you speak. __________
Explain your answer. ____
____
____

8. Use hand or body gestures to explain size or distance or to dramatize a point. __________
Explain your answer. ______________________
____
____
____
____
____

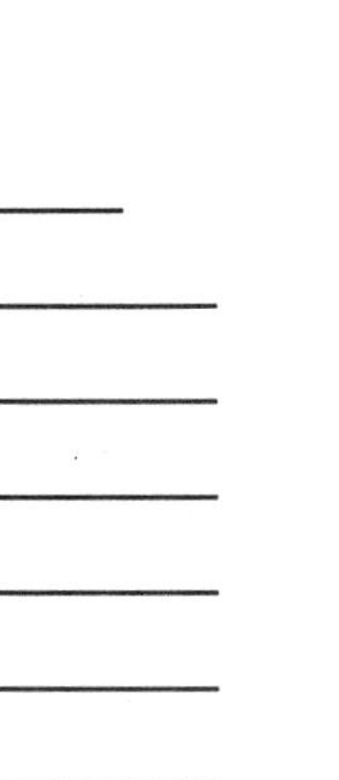

9. Comb your hair, dress neatly, and come to school well rested on the day of your speech. __________
Explain your answer. ______________________
____
____
____
____
____

If you have trouble looking at the audience, look just above their heads. They won't even notice!

Name ______________________________

Adding Fun Elements

When you add fun, interesting elements to oral presentations, you get the audience's attention and make your presentation fun to hear.

Directions

Read the oral-presentation subjects. Think of a fun photograph, an illustration, a grid, a diagram, a chart, a prop, or a demonstration that could be used to make each presentation more interesting and informative.

Be careful! You don't want the "fun stuff" to distract the audience from your speech!

Oral Presentation Subject		Fun Element
Alexander Graham Bell (inventor of the telephone)		
The Evolution of the Car		
How We Use Computers in Our Everyday Lives		
My Favorite Movie		
My Family Tree		
Water and Its Phases (Steam, Water, Ice)		

ARE YOU A PRECISE, EFFICIENT REPORT WRITER?

To write good reports, you need to write precisely and efficiently to share ideas. Are you a precise, efficient writer? Take the following survey to find out.

Name ______________________________

Directions

Read each statement and circle a number from 0–4. Total your points and check your score at the bottom to see how well you write reports.

0 = never **1 = occasionally** **2 = sometimes** **3 = often** **4 = always**

	Statement					
1	I ask my teacher the "right" questions to find out the requirements for a report.	**0**	**1**	**2**	**3**	**4**
2	I know how to gather facts from books and computers for my report.	**0**	**1**	**2**	**3**	**4**
3	I brainstorm before I write.	**0**	**1**	**2**	**3**	**4**
4	I organize report facts on note cards and in an outline.	**0**	**1**	**2**	**3**	**4**
5	I carefully write my rough draft.	**0**	**1**	**2**	**3**	**4**
6	I check my rough draft for spelling, punctuation, and grammatical errors.	**0**	**1**	**2**	**3**	**4**
7	I read my rough draft aloud or invite a friend or family member to read it.	**0**	**1**	**2**	**3**	**4**
8	I carefully write my final draft in my best handwriting (or use my best keyboarding skills).	**0**	**1**	**2**	**3**	**4**
9	I add "finishing touches" such as a title page, illustrations, diagrams, and a cover.	**0**	**1**	**2**	**3**	**4**

If you scored

- **30 or above,** *congratulations! You've got the "write" stuff; get ready to learn some more.*
- **19–29,** *right on! With just a few more tips, your writing will be "write" on the money!*
- **10–18,** *you need some help getting on the "write" track. Pay attention to the upcoming techniques.*
- **0–9,** *pay close attention "write" away!*

Name ______________________________

Getting the Facts

To be a smart report writer, ask questions to get as much information as possible before you begin the assignment.

Directions

Read the report description and answer the questions on this page and page 71. Keep this page so you can ask the same questions when you are assigned a "real" report.

Report Description for Reading Class

You have been assigned to write a report about a favorite athlete. It is due two weeks from today's date. The report should be at least three pages long. The report can be handwritten or typed. It should be single spaced with a double space between paragraphs. Page numbers should appear at the bottom center of each page. The report should be placed in a folder and should include at least one illustration. You should have a bibliography with at least two sources.

1. In which class has the report been assigned? ______________________
2. What is the subject of the report? ______________________________
3. When is the report due? ______________________
4. What form of writing should be used?
   a. handwritten
   b. typed
   c. handwritten or typed
   d. other ______________________________

Sometimes completed reports will become oral presentations. Be sure to ask!

Name ___________________________

5. What spacing should be used?
   a. single spaced
   b. single spaced with a double space between paragraphs
   c. double spaced
   d. other _______________

6. How should the pages be numbered?
   a. top left of the page
   b. top center of the page
   c. top right of the page
   d. bottom left of the page
   e. bottom center of the page
   f. bottom right of the page

7. Should the report be in a folder?
   a. yes
   b. no

8. Should the report include photographs, illustrations, or a chart?
   a. yes
   b. no

9. Should the report have a bibliography?
   a. yes
   b. no

10. If the report has a bibliography, how many sources are needed?

____

Name ______________________

Prewriting

Before you write a report, think about what you already know. Then you should brainstorm what you want to know and what you want your reader to learn.

Directions

Choose a subject for a report you would like to write. Read the heading for each section of the prewriting grid and brainstorm ideas. Write your ideas using words, phrases, sentences, dates, symbols, and/or acronyms.

REPORT SUBJECT: ______________________

What I Already Know about the Subject	What I Want to Know about the Subject	What I Want My Reader to Feel or Learn

Organize the grid before you write. You can write an outline or make a list to show the order in which you will write your ideas and facts.

Name ______________________________

Using Reference Materials

Reference books are great for finding information for a report. If you use reference books often and well, you can write very informative reports!

Directions

Use the listed reference books to find the answers to the following questions.

When you use a reference book, be sure to write down the title, author's name, publishing company, page number, and date of publication.

Reference Book Choices: **thesaurus** **atlas** **dictionary** **encyclopedia** **almanac**

1. What are three synonyms for *happy?* ______________________________
2. Who won Super Bowl XXXI? ______________________________
3. How do you pronounce *cerebellum?* ______________________________
4. In 1991, what was the approximate population of San Juan, Argentina? ______________________________
5. Where is Tanzania? ______________________________
6. Which American woman won the Nobel Peace Prize in 1997? ______________________________
7. How does a submarine submerge? ______________________________
8. On what continent is the country of Poland? ______________________________
9. What is an antonym for *tiny?* ______________________________
10. What is the life cycle of the butterfly? ______________________________

Name ______________________________

Preparing Note Cards

You can use note cards to organize the information you gather for a report. Note cards help you sort information that will become subjects for paragraphs.

Directions

Read the sample note card. Then read the directions to create your own note card on the index card below.

(Habitat) **Countries of Origin**
Vampire bats are found in Central and South America, including Mexico, Chile, Argentina, the islands of Trinidad and Margarita, and Venezuela.
Vampire Bats by Chris Gorsky, p. 75
Looking Glass Publishers, 1998

Pretend you are writing a report about vampire bats. Use an encyclopedia as your reference and prepare a note card that gives one fact about a vampire bat's body.

Sort completed note cards into categories by subject. Sequence each pile of cards to show the order in which you will write the information. Transfer the information to an outline before you write a rough draft.

Name ____________________

Making an Outline from Note Cards

It's usually best to write an outline based on your note cards so you know the order in which you want to write your report.

Directions

Read the note cards below and write their titles and facts in the correct order on the outline on page 76.

Outlines are easy to write if you've sorted and titled your note cards!

(Challenges) **Physical Challenges**

Contracted ophthalmia, an eye infection that blinded one eye

(Childhood) **Where She Lived**

Moved to New York in 1832, to New Jersey in 1835, and to Ohio in 1838

(Education) **College**

Accepted to Geneva Collge in 1848

(Childhood) **Birth**

Born in Bristol, England

(Accomplishments) **Why Important**

Became first woman to receive a medical degree in the U.S.

Name ____________________

Directions

Read the note cards on page 75 and write their titles and facts in the correct order on the following outline.

TITLE: ELIZABETH BLACKWELL

I. Accomplishments

A. ____________________

1. ____________________

____

B. How She Helped Others

1. Wrote papers on the importance of good hygiene
2. Opened an infirmary especially for women and children
3. Established the Women's Medical College of New York in 1868

II. Childhood

A. ____________________

1. ____________________
2. In 1821

B. ____________________

1. ____________________

____

2. Stayed in Ohio until she got a teaching job in Kentucky

III. Education

A. Elementary School

1. In England until she was 11
2. In New York City until she was 12

B. Secondary School

1. At home with her mother as teacher

C. ____________________

1. ____________________
2. La Maternité in Paris, France
3. St. Bartholomew School of Medicine in England

IV. Challenges

A. Challenges from Others

1. Was turned down by several medical schools including Harvard
2. No institution in the United States would hire her after she got her M.D.

B. ____________________

1. ____________________

____

2. Fell in 1907, never recovered, and died in 1910 as a result

Name ______________________________

Rough Drafts

Once you've gathered report information and created an outline, you're ready to write a rough draft. For this draft, write the information in your own words.

Directions

Read a rough draft you've recently written and grade it by giving yourself a letter grade *(A, B, C, D,* or *F)* for each line on the following report card. From now on, when you write a rough draft for a report, think about each important element.

Rough Draft Report Card	Grade
1 My opening paragraph introduced the main idea of the report.	________
2 My opening paragraph was interesting so the reader would want to keep reading.	________
3 Each paragraph in the body of the report dealt with only one subject.	________
4 Each paragraph had a good topic sentence.	________
5 The information in each paragraph was written in a logical order.	________
6 The closing paragraph summarized the information presented in the report.	________
7 The paragraphs were placed in a logical order so the report made sense.	________
8 I used my own words rather than copy them from a book.	________
9 My last sentence let the reader know that the paper was finished.	________

Don't worry when you write a rough draft! The most important thing is to write your ideas (in your own words) in a logical, interesting way.

Name ______________________

Editing

After you write your rough draft, it's time to take out the red pen and check, check, check! The more you edit, the less mistakes you'll have in your final draft.

Directions

Read a rough draft you have recently written. Use the following guide to check your rough draft. Check off each item when you have completed it. Then use this guide each time you write a rough draft.

Editing Guide

- [ ] 1 My report has an appropriate title and is labeled correctly.
- [ ] 2 The opening paragraph is interesting and introduces the main idea of the report.
- [ ] 3 All paragraphs begin with a good topic sentence.
- [ ] 4 All sentences are complete.
- [ ] 5 Each paragraph in the body of the report deals with one subject only and is written in a logical order.
- [ ] 6 The closing paragraph summarizes the information presented in the report.
- [ ] 7 The paragraphs are placed in a logical order so the report makes sense.
- [ ] 8 I use my own words, not words copied from a book.
- [ ] 9 I use "strong" verbs and interesting adjectives when appropriate.
- [ ] 10 I use similes, metaphors, and other descriptive language when appropriate.
- [ ] 11 My last sentence lets the reader know that the paper is finished.
- [ ] 12 I use capital letters in the correct places.
- [ ] 13 I use correct punctuation (periods, commas, question marks, apostrophes, quotation marks, and exclamation marks).
- [ ] 14 I have changed all spelling errors by looking up the words in a dictionary or by using the "spell check" on the computer.

Read the report aloud to check for mistakes. Then have a friend or family member read it.

Name ______________________________

Final Drafts

The final draft is your last chance to write the best report possible.
If you look at your final draft and see your best work, you should feel very proud.

Directions

Complete the crossword puzzle for tips on preparing a final draft that any student would be proud of.

Across

1. Complete a b_____________ of reference sources if one is required.
4. Carefully copy your edited rough draft word for w________.
6. Write a final draft in your best h_____________.
7. To add the finishing touches, create a t_______ page, a cover, and an illustration or a diagram to go with your report.
9. Change all m____________ that you found in your paper before turning it in.

Across

2. R______ your final draft when you are done to check for mistakes.
3. Type your report on a c_________________ if you have one and if your teacher approves.
5. I___________ (move the beginning over two finger spaces) all paragraphs.
8. Be sure to l________ your paper with your name, the title, the date, and the name of the class in which it is due.

You will copy your final draft more accurately if you take your time and work in a quiet, well-lit space.

Name ______________________________

Finishing Touches

When you add interesting finishing touches to reports, you get to express the information you learned in a fun, unique way.

Directions

Read the research report subjects. Think of a graph, an illustration, a grid, a diagram, or a chart that could be used to make the report more interesting and informative.

Don't forget to complete the finishing touches neatly!

Report Subject	Finishing Touch
Dinosaurs 	
The American Revolution 	
The History of Flight 	
Peggy Fleming (Figure Skater) 	
The Indian Elephant 	
Zaire 	

DO YOU HAVE A GOOD MEMORY?

Do you know how to study so you remember information well? Take the following survey to find out.

Name ______________________________

Directions

Read each statement and circle a number from 0–4. (If you don't know what something is, mark 0.) Total your points and check your score at the bottom to see how well you use memory builders.

0 = never **1 = occasionally** **2 = sometimes** **3 = often** **4 = always**

1	I use acronyms to remember information.	0	1	2	3	4
2	I use acrostics to remember information.	0	1	2	3	4
3	I visualize funny pictures to remember information.	0	1	2	3	4
4	I draw pictures to remember information.	0	1	2	3	4
5	I use flip cards to remember vocabulary and other facts.	0	1	2	3	4
6	I make up songs to remember information.	0	1	2	3	4
7	I make up rhymes to remember information.	0	1	2	3	4
8	I have a system to remember dates.	0	1	2	3	4
9	I see patterns in numbers.	0	1	2	3	4

If you scored

- **33 or above,** *congratulations! You have the skills to build an incredible memory!*
- **28–32,** *you remember things quite well. Learn some new tricks and you'll raise your score!*
- **18–27,** *it's time for a little memory improvement. Pay attention to the upcoming tips and you'll be amazed.*
- **0–17,** *it's time to learn some memory tricks!*

Name ______________________

Acronyms

A good way to remember information is to create an acronym. You use a letter from each word in the information you want to remember and create a new word that stands for it.

Directions

Read the acronym example and the information that follows. Then create your own acronym for each piece of information. If you have trouble making a "real word," invent a nonsense word that sounds as if it could be real. (You can add a vowel if you need one.)

Example: SCUBA stands for **s**elf-**c**ontained **u**nderwater **b**reathing **a**pparatus.

1. Make an acronym to remember the names of the seven continents: North America, South America, Europe, Africa, Asia, Australia, Antarctica.

Acronym: ______________________

2. Make an acronym to remember the three types of triangles: scalene, isosceles, equilateral.

Acronym: ______________________

3. Make an acronym to remember the five main parts of the eye: cornea, iris, pupil, lens, retina.

Acronym: ______________________

4. Make an acronym for the names of the first three presidents (keep these words in order): George Washington, John Adams, Thomas Jefferson.

Acronym: ______________________

5. Make an acronym for the names of the five brightest stars: Alpha Centauri, Sirius, Procyon, Altair, Fomalhaut.

Acronym: ______________________

In everyday life, you can use acronyms to remember grocery lists.

Name ____________________

Acrostics

An acrostic is a sentence that uses the first letter from each word you want to remember and substitutes a word using the same letter. Acrostics are great when you have to remember information in a certain order.

Directions

Read the acrostic example and the information that follows. Then create your own acrostic for each piece of information. If you have trouble making a sentence, add words such as *a* or *the*.

Example: The planets in our solar system are **M**ercury, **V**enus, **E**arth, **M**ars, **J**upiter, **S**aturn, **U**ranus, **N**eptune, and **P**luto.

Acrostic: My **V**ery **E**ducated **M**other **J**ust **S**ent **U**s **N**ine **P**izzas.

1. Create an acrostic for the colors in the spectrum: red, orange, yellow, green, blue, indigo, violet.

Acrostic: ____________________

____

2. Create an acrostic for the minerals in Mohs Scale of Hardness (from softest to hardest): talc, gypsum, calcite, fluorite, apatite, feldspar, quartz, topaz, corundum, diamond.

Acrostic: ____________________

____

3. Create an acrostic for the states in New England: Maine, Vermont, New Hampshire, Massachusetts, Connecticut, Rhode Island.

Acrostic: ____________________

____

Try to keep your acrostics simple. Silly acrostics can be easy to remember, too!

Name ______________________

Pictures in Your Mind

A great way to remember a list of words is to create a funny picture in your mind that links all the words together.

Directions

Read the example and look at its picture. Then read the word lists, create a picture in your mind for each list, and draw sketches to show the pictures.

Example

Shopping List

bread, eggs, carrots, butter, apples, lettuce

Making pictures in your mind works best for short lists of words.

1. Shopping List

toothbrush, toothpaste, floss, soap, shampoo, comb, brush

2. Homework Supplies

paper, pencil, calculator, watch, book, snack

Name ______________________________

Drawing Sketches

Another great way to remember facts is to draw a simple sketch that symbolizes the information, and then memorize that picture.

Directions

Read the example and look at its picture. Then read the word lists and draw a sketch for each one.

Example: On July 20, 1969, Neil Armstrong and Buzz Aldrin became the first people to walk on the Moon.

Try to keep the pictures simple. Complicated pictures waste time and are hard to remember. Pictures help when you're taking notes, too!

1 The Boston Tea Party was staged in December 1773, as a protest to tea and sugar taxes.	**3** The hydrosphere (Earth's surface covered with water) makes up 71% of Earth. The lithosphere (dry land) makes up 29%.
2 Mark Twain (Samuel Clemens), who wrote *The Adventures of Tom Sawyer*, lived from 1835 to 1910.	**4** A solar eclipse occurs when the moon's shadow is cast on Earth as it passes directly between the Sun and Earth.

Name ______________________________

Flip Books

When you need to remember vocabulary or answers to specific questions, you can make a flip book to remember the information.

Directions

Follow the directions below to make a flip book for a current list of vocabulary words and definitions.

1. Use an index card for each word, and punch a hole in the top-left corner of each card.
2. Tie the cards together with a piece of yarn.
3. Write a vocabulary word on each card. Write the definition on the back.
4. Read and spell the first word. Try to remember the definition you wrote and say it. Turn the card over to see if you are correct. If you are, move the card to the right. If you are incorrect, move the card to the left.

5. Go through each word.
6. Play the game until you can name each definition on the first try.
7. Turn the cards over and play the game the other way. Read the definitions and try to name and spell the words.

Flip books are great for math facts, too!

Name ______________________

Songs

Another good way to remember information is to use a familiar tune and write a song that incorporates what needs to be remembered.

Directions

Read the example. Then use one of the suggested tunes to write your own song for the multiplication facts of eight.

Example: Whistle While You Learn
(to the tune of "Whistle While You Work")

Whistle while you learn (whistle)
and musically together we will learn the facts of nine.
9 x 9 is 81. I think this could be fun.
72 is 9 x 8. Hey, this is really great.
9 x 7 is 63. I sound smart as can be.
54 is 9 x 6. I like these little tricks.
9 x 5 is 45. These facts are starting to jive.
36 is 9 x 4. I like this even more.
The last four that remain
Are easy just the same.
Just match these answers to the facts
To end this rhyming game.
9 x 3 is 27.
9 x 2 is 18.
9 x 1 is 9.
9 x 0 is 0.

Always choose an easy-to-remember tune!

Tune Suggestions

"Are You Sleeping?"'
"Old MacDonald"
"London Bridge"
"Yankee Doodle"
"The Farmer in the Dell"
"Jingle Bells"

My Song for the Multiplication Facts of Eight

Name ______________________________

Rhymes

Sometimes making up simple rhymes is the easiest way to commit single pieces of information (such as definitions) to memory.

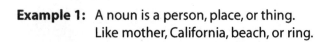

Directions

Read the examples. Then make up your own rhymes for the information presented.

Example 1: A noun is a person, place, or thing.
Like mother, California, beach, or ring.

Example 2: An adjective is a word that describes a noun.
Like old, silly, tired, or round.

1. An adverb adds meaning to the verb in a phrase.

____

2. A verb is called an action word.

____

3. My state has a capital, yes it's true.

____

4. There are many kinds of fish in the sea.

____

5. Water is called H_2O.

____

6. My school's phone number is easy to say.

____

Always write down your rhymes so you can practice them.

Name ______________________________

Time Lines

Do you know how to remember a lot of dates and events in a row?
Read on to learn how to use time lines to put important dates "in your head."

Directions

When you need to remember a series of dates in order, use a time line as a memory helper. Read the example and then draw your own time line using the facts below.

Example: The Battleship *Bismarck*

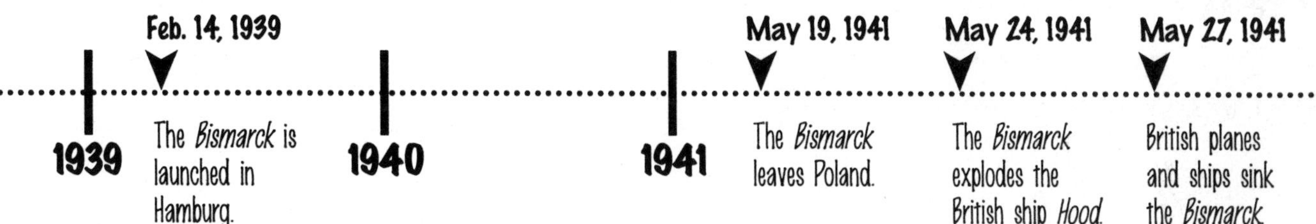

Feb. 14, 1939
The Bismarck is launched in Hamburg.
1939
1940
1941
May 19, 1941
The Bismarck leaves Poland.
May 24, 1941
The Bismarck explodes the British ship Hood.
May 27, 1941
British planes and ships sink the Bismarck.

Facts

April 6, 1917
The U.S. enters World War I.

June 28, 1914
Archduke Ferdinand is assassinated.

May 7, 1915
The *Lusitania* is sunk.

November 11, 1918
World War I ends.

July 28, 1914
World War I starts.

WORLD WAR I

1914
1915
1916
1917
1918

Name ______________________________

Remembering Dates with Rhymes

If you only have to remember one date and a little information that goes with it, use a rhyme to help you remember. It's quick, easy, and fun!

Directions

Read the rhyming example and then make your own rhymes using the dates below.

At Kitty Hawk, in 1903, Orville Wright went on a flying spree.

Try this strategy to remember birthdays. It works!

Example: In 1492, Columbus sailed to a world that was new.

1. The Boston Tea Party took place in 1773.

____

2. The Civil War began in 1861.

____

3. Neil Armstrong walked on the moon in 1969.

____

4. Chief Joseph became chief of the Nez Percé Indians in 1871.

____

5. Marie Curie, the Polish physicist, was born on November 7, 1867.

____

6. Women in the United States were given the right to vote on August 18, 1920.

____

Name ______________________________

Remembering Numbers

When you can remember numbers and math facts, you save time and can complete more complex problems.

Directions

Try the following techniques to remember math facts and operations. Check off each technique after you try it. Use these ideas when you study for math tests.

☐ **1** To memorize math facts, make a set of flash cards with the problems on one side and the answers on the other. Quiz yourself several times or have a friend quiz you until you know the facts quickly and accurately.

☐ **2** Tape-record yourself reciting math facts or the order of math operations. Put on earphones and play the tape whenever you travel or have free time.

☐ **3** Look for and remember repeating patterns in numbers. Below are two examples of repeating number patterns. Study to remember these patterns and then look for more as you complete math assignments.

Example 1: The Nine Trick

When multiplying by 9, you can add the two digits of the answer together. The answer will always be 9. If you get another number when you add the digits, you know your answer is wrong.

9 x 2 = **18** (**1** + **8** = 9)
9 x 3 = **27** (**2** + **7** = 9)
9 x 4 = **36** (**3** + **6** = 9)
9 x 5 = **45** (**4** + **5** = 9)
9 x 6 = **54** (**5** + **4** = 9)
9 x 7 = **63** (**6** + **3** = 9)
9 x 8 = **72** (**7** + **2** = 9)
9 x 9 = **81** (**8** + **1** = 9)

Example 2: The Three Trick

When multiplying by 3, you can add the two digits of the answer together. The answers will always follow a pattern (3, 6, 9). If you get another number when you add the digits, you know your answer is wrong.

3 x 1 = **3** (**3**)
3 x 2 = **6** (**6**)
3 x 3 = **9** (**9**)
3 x 4 = **12** (1 + 2 = **3**)
3 x 5 = **15** (1 + 5 = **6**)
3 x 6 = **18** (1 + 8 = **9**)
3 x 7 = **21** (2 + 1 = **3**)
3 x 8 = **24** (2 + 4 = **6**)
3 x 9 = **27** (2 + 7 = **9**)

Because math skills build on each other, it's important to memorize basic addition, subtraction, multiplication, and division facts so you can do harder problems later.

Name ____________________

Group Games

Sometimes it's easier to memorize information if you play study games with a group of friends or family.

Directions

With a group of friends, choose one of the following games. Play the game using information from a current chapter in a textbook.

Game 1: Team Q & A

Divide your group into two teams. Meet with your team and use information from your chapter to write several questions and answers. At the same time, have the other team write questions for your team to answer. Ask the other team your questions and award points for correct answers. Then have the other team ask their questions while your team tries to answer.

Game 2: Twenty Questions

Have each person from your group choose an event or person from your chapter to study. (Show all the choices to someone who isn't in your group to check that no two people have the same event or person.) After studying, choose one person to be "it" first. Have the rest of the group ask "it" *yes* or *no* questions to get information and guess the event or person. If the group can't guess within 20 questions, have "it" tell the answer. Play until everyone has a turn to be "it."

Game 3: Draw It

Divide your group into two teams. Meet with your team and write the names of five or six events or people on separate index cards. At the same time, have the other team write five or six names. (Show all the cards to someone who isn't in your group to check that both teams have different events or people.) Have a person from the other team choose one of your team's cards and draw picture clues about the event or person on the card. The "drawer's" team should look at the pictures and try to guess the event or person. If the other team guesses correctly within one minute, they get a point. Have your team take the next turn to draw and guess. Take turns until all the cards are used.

Sometimes there is a temptation to "goof off" when you study with friends. Try your best to concentrate!

DO YOU KNOW HOW TO STUDY FOR A TEST?

The time spent before a test is critical to your success during the test. Do you know the best ways to study for tests? Take the following survey to find out.

Name ______________________________

Directions

Read each statement and circle a number from 0–4. Total your points and check your score at the bottom to see how well you prepare for tests.

0 = never **1 = occasionally** **2 = sometimes** **3 = often** **4 = always**

	Statement					
1	I have a good "game plan" so I can make the most of my study time.	0	1	2	3	4
2	I find out about review sessions.	0	1	2	3	4
3	I ask about the kind of test and if the questions will come from notes, textbooks, or both.	0	1	2	3	4
4	I use memory-building techniques when I study.	0	1	2	3	4
5	I know the dates of all my tests so I can plan ahead.	0	1	2	3	4
6	I know how to study alone.	0	1	2	3	4
7	I know how to study with a partner.	0	1	2	3	4
8	I know how to study with a group.	0	1	2	3	4

If you scored

- **25 or above,** *congratulations! You're a "study machine"! Get ready for some more tips to make "getting ready" even easier!*
- **17–24,** *good job. Now get ready to make your score even better!*
- **9–16,** *use the upcoming suggestions and you'll get better test grades!.*
- **0–8,** *it's time for the learning to begin. Pay attention to the upcoming tips!*

Name ______________________

Game Plan

You should have a game plan for a test. In other words, you should know what to do before and during a test to make sure you get the best grade possible.

Directions

Choose one "start" box at the top of the maze on page 95 and draw a line through the maze to show the best "game plan" for taking a test.

If you follow the correct path on the maze and follow the directions in real life, you'll be *amazed* at your improvement!

Name ____________________

Read each box and draw a line through the best choices to make your way through the maze.

START	START	START	START
Start: Whatever you do, don't ask questions.	**Start:** Daydream about soccer.	**Start:** Find out the date of the test.	**Start:** Draw doodles.
Take a nap in class.	Ask if there will be a review session.	Find out the kind of test: true or false, multiple choice, etc.	Count ceiling tiles.
Read your favorite magazine.	Ask if the questions will be taken from notes or a book.	Finish your homework.	Pass notes to a friend.
Get a snack.	Ask how long you will have to complete the test.	Begin studying. Reread chapters and notes. Write down key information.	Use memory-building techniques to memorize key information.
Watch TV while you study a second time.	Quit studying; you already studied once.	Study with a partner.	Make up and take a practice test or write an outline.
It's test time. Read ahead and start the test before the teacher has given instructions.	It's test time. Don't listen because you won't know the answers anyway.	It's test time. Listen to the teacher's instructions.	It's test time. Daydream about the test being over.
Skip the directions and get started!	Read the directions carefully. Circle or underline important parts.	Begin at the easiest section. If you get stuck, skip the question and mark it.	Do the hardest section first and keep working on it until you are done.
Circle or write in any answer. You still might pass.	Copy from a classmate.	Have a panic attack, start to sweat, and get blurred vision so you can't read the questions.	Go back and answer all questions, keeping your eye on the time.
End: Look at your classmate's paper to see if you have the same answers.	**End:** Turn in your test without double-checking.	**End:** Double-check your answers and then turn in your test.	**End:** Turn in your test and throw paper wads.

Name ____________________

Studying Alone

Most people find it best to study alone for a test first and then later with a partner or group.

Directions

Read the following "studying alone" tips and then use them as you follow the directions to the right.

Tip 1

Study alone in a comfortable place that has good lighting and plenty of materials.

Tip 2

Study alone at a time of day when you feel most awake.

Tip 3

Take as long as you need to complete the task, but take breaks when you need them.

Tip 4

Use techniques such as acronyms and acrostics to help you remember.

Use the above tips to memorize the spelling and definition of each of the following words. After you study, have a friend quiz you to see if you can spell each word and write its definition. On the back of this paper, write a paragraph to explain how you did on the quiz and which tips worked best for you.

1. mellow (adjective)
   ripe, well matured; gentle, pleasant
2. lethargic (adjective)
   unnaturally sleepy; dull, slow moving
3. random (adjective)
   by chance, not planned or prearranged; irregular

Don't "cram" the night before a test. Study alone a little each night so studying will be "more review and less new"!

Name ______________________________

Studying with a Partner

Studying with a partner can really help you remember information.
When you seriously study with a partner, you can really improve your performance.

Directions

Read the following "studying with a partner" tips and then use them when you follow the directions to the left.

Tip 1

Choose one partner and set a specific date and time to study.

Tip 2

Study in a place where you won't be disturbed.

Tip 3

Take time to review information together, share notes, and read aloud to each other.

Tip 4

Quiz each other on the reviewed information. If you or your partner do not do well on the quiz, review and quiz again until both of you know the information.

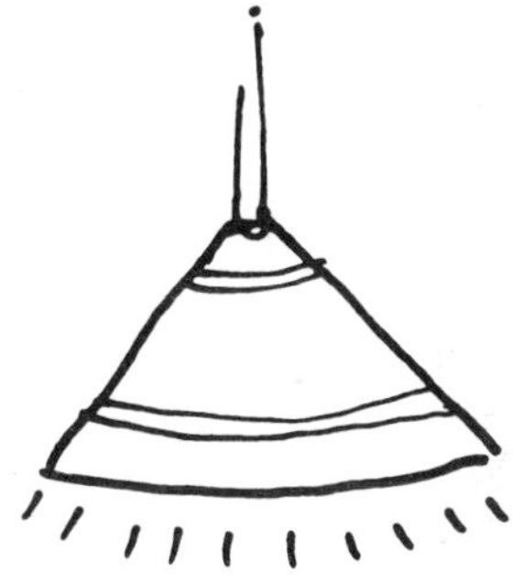

Use the above tips to memorize the spelling and definition of each of the following words. After you study, have your partner quiz you to see if you can spell each word and write its definition. On the back of this paper, write a paragraph to explain how you did on the quiz and which tips worked best for you.

1. harmonious (adjective)
   able to get along well together

2. sagacious (adjective)
   shrewd; wise in a keen, practical way

3. hardy (adjective)
   able to survive through difficult conditions

It's best to study with someone who cares about learning. Avoid studying with a "goof-off."

Name ______________________

Studying in a Group

Studying with a group is great for a "just before the test" review session.
Groups can brainstorm ideas for answers to essay or fill-in-the-blank questions, too.

Directions

Meet with a group of three of four friends and think of six "ground rules" to follow when you study together. Read the examples to get started and then write your own. When all the group lists are done, discuss them as a class and come up with one set of "class rules."

Study/slumber parties the night before a test are usually not a good idea!

Example 1: Study with a group after you have studied alone.

Example 2: End your study session if there is more goofing off than studying.

1. ______________________
2. ______________________
3. ______________________
4. ______________________
5. ______________________
6. ______________________

ARE YOU A GOOD TEST-TAKER?

There are many strategies to help you do well on tests.
Do you know and use them? Take the following survey to find out.

Name ______________________________

Directions

Read each statement and circle a number from 0–4. Total your points and check your score at the bottom to see how well you take tests.

0 = never 1 = occasionally 2 = sometimes 3 = often 4 = always

1	I listen to the teacher's instructions just before a test.	0	1	2	3	4
2	I read and underline key words in directions.	0	1	2	3	4
3	I do easy parts of the test first and then go back to the hard parts.	0	1	2	3	4
4	I answer all the questions, even if I have to make a guess.	0	1	2	3	4
5	I look for key words on matching tests.	0	1	2	3	4
6	I read all possible choices before marking an answer on a multiple-choice test.	0	1	2	3	4
7	I use the process of elimination on multiple-choice tests.	0	1	2	3	4
8	I read true-or-false statements carefully and look for "tricks."	0	1	2	3	4
9	On true-or-false tests, I look for words that indicate either a true or a false statement.	0	1	2	3	4
10	I brainstorm and outline before I write an essay.	0	1	2	3	4
11	I restate the teacher's question when I begin an essay.	0	1	2	3	4
12	I check all my answers before I turn in my work.	0	1	2	3	4

If you scored

- **40 or above,** *congratulations! You're a good test-taker, aren't you? Want to be a great one? Get ready!*
- **30–39,** *keep it up. You'll do even better with the upcoming tips.*
- **20–29,** *take some time to study the upcoming techniques and you'll do great on your next test.*
- **0–19,** *it's time to take tests more seriously and learn from the upcoming tips!*

Name ___________________________

Underlining Key Words

As you read directions, you should underline key words so you understand exactly what to do. Review the underlined words during the test if you forget the instructions.

Directions

Carefully read the following directions. Underline key words in the directions and then do what the directions describe.

Don't be afraid to ask the teacher for help with understanding directions. Your teacher wants you to do well!

1. Place punctuation marks where they are needed in the following sentence. Circle each word that should begin with a capital letter.
   - arizonas state flower is the giant cactus

2. Write *no* after the group of words that is not a sentence. Write *yes* after the group of words that is a sentence.
   - Over there where the coral was so beautiful.
   - My sister loves to dance.

3. Draw one line under the noun in the following sentence and two lines under the verb.
   - The moon shone brightly.

4. Circle the word in parentheses that correctly fits in the sentence.
   - You can see the moon (clearly, clear) tonight.

5. Column A lists two words. Column B lists their definitions. After each word in Column A, write the letter of its definition.

A.	B.
1. weak ___________	a. seven days
2. week ___________	b. without strength

Name ______________________________

Reading Test Directions

To be a smart test-taker, you should read directions carefully before the test and then reread them during the test if you need help.

Directions

Pretend the following directions are real test directions. Carefully read and follow the directions to take the test below.

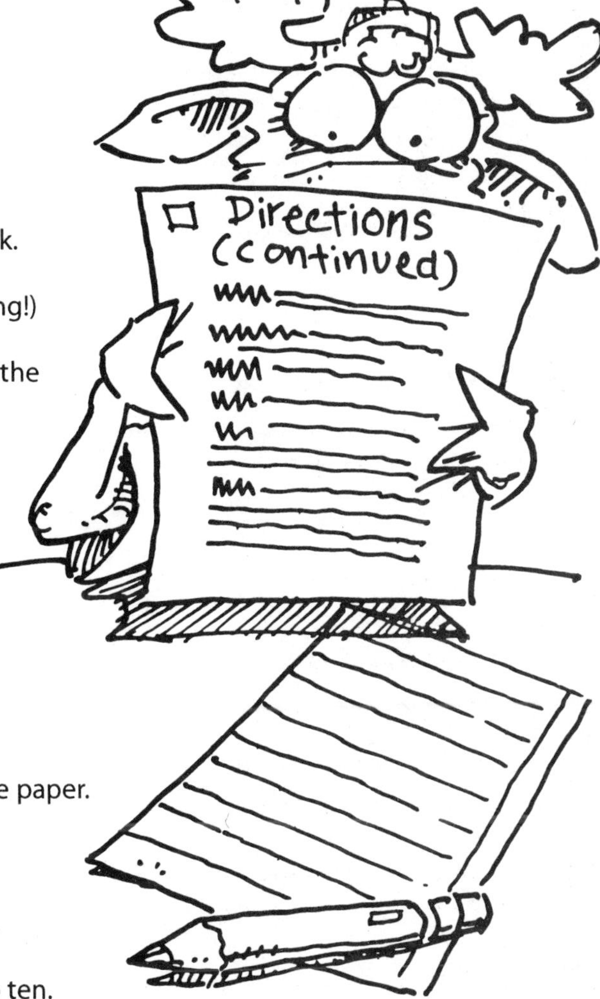

1. Do not write on the front of this paper. Write on the back.
2. Read all the directions before doing anything. (No erasing!)
3. Put your name, your best friend's name, and the date in the upper right-hand corner of the paper.
4. Draw a flower with five large petals in the middle of your paper.
5. In each flower petal, draw a triangle.
6. Draw a stem and one leaf on your flower.
7. Scratch your head.
8. Write your birthdate in the lower left-hand corner of the paper.
9. Stand up, turn around, and sit down.
10. Under the flower, write the name of your favorite sport.
11. Under the sport's name, write the numbers from one to ten.
12. In the upper left-hand corner of the paper, draw a tree.
13. If you followed the directions perfectly so far, write an *A* at the top of your paper.
14. Now that you have finished reading all the directions, go back and follow only the directions for numbers 3, 4, and 10.

STUDY BUDDY TIP: Never lean over to ask a friend about directions. You don't want to look like you're cheating.

Name ____________________

Checking Math Tests

Always check your math work. One mistake in a single step can make a whole answer wrong. Pace yourself during tests to leave time for checking your work.

Directions

Read the three checking systems at the right. Then complete the following math problems. Use the three systems to check each problem.

System 1

Go back and check the sign in the operation. Were you supposed to add or subtract? Multiply or divide? Make sure you did what the problem asked.

System 2

Right after you complete a problem, do it again in your head to make sure you did it correctly.

System 3

Check each problem in reverse. Start at the bottom (with the answer), reverse the sign (such as from addition to subtraction), and do the problem so the middle number remains in place and the top number becomes the answer.

Do these problems and use each checking system. As you try out System 3, write a new problem next to each original problem.

486	1,463	885
+359	− 858	x 9

Form your numbers as neatly as possible. A messy correct answer may be mistaken for a wrong answer. Give it your best!

Name ______________________________

Matching Tests

A matching test is a "recognition test"; the test-taker needs to recognize the answers, not memorize them. Approach matching tests in the following way so you can best recognize the answers.

Directions

Read the statements below and choose the answer for each statement from the choices at the right. Write the corresponding letter next to each statement. If your answers are correct, you should write a sentence vertically.

Be sure to ask if an answer can be used twice.

1. ______Always write this on your paper first.
2. ______Read directions this way.
3. ______Find out if the answers can be used like this.
4. ______Always write this type of letter clearly so your writing is not misunderstood.
5. ______Look for these words in the statements or questions.
6. ______Don't do this unless you are positive of the answer.
7. ______If you are asked to draw lines from one side of the page to the other, draw them this way at first so you can erase and change your answers. When you are done, draw the lines boldly.

T. faintly

O. capital

G. your name

R. key

O. carefully

F. more than once

I. cross out "used" answers

Write the sentence you made here: ______________________________!

Name ____________________

Multiple-Choice Tests

Multiple-choice tests are "recognition tests"; you need to recognize answers, not memorize them. Use the following strategies for help with multiple-choice tests.

Directions

Read the following multiple-choice statements and circle the best answer for each statement. Write the corresponding letter above its number at the bottom of the page. If your choices are correct, you should write a sentence.

Multiple-choice questions can be worded to make you think very hard. Always study hard for tests and read the questions carefully.

1 Before reading directions, you should
- d. listen to the teacher's instructions.
- f. have all supplies ready.
- t. write your name on your paper.
- o. all of the above.

2 You should always read the directions
- a. carefully.
- s. last.
- c. quickly.
- v. out loud.

3 You should always read
- e. all the answer choices before making a decision.
- w. the answer choices until you find the right answer.
- p. none of the answers; just circle one.
- l. the first and last answers only.

4 Read the questions and answer choices to find the
- b. quickest answer.
- k. inappropriate answer.
- m. best answer.
- j. silliest answer.

5 If you can't decide on the correct answer, you should
- r. cross out the answers you know are wrong.
- i. cross out the answers that are probably wrong.
- p. make a decision from the answers you have not crossed out.
- y. all of the above.

6 Many times the correct answer is
- b. the longer, more detailed answer.
- n. "all of the above."
- v. obvious if you studied.
- k. all of the above.

7 To make the best use of your time, you should
- f. read as quickly as possible.
- s. skip the questions for which you don't know the answers and go back to them later.
- g. circle any answer.
- n. look at the clock every other minute.

8 You should always go back and
- a. double-check your work.
- h. carefully erase changed answers.
- k. mark an answer for every question.
- d. all of the above.

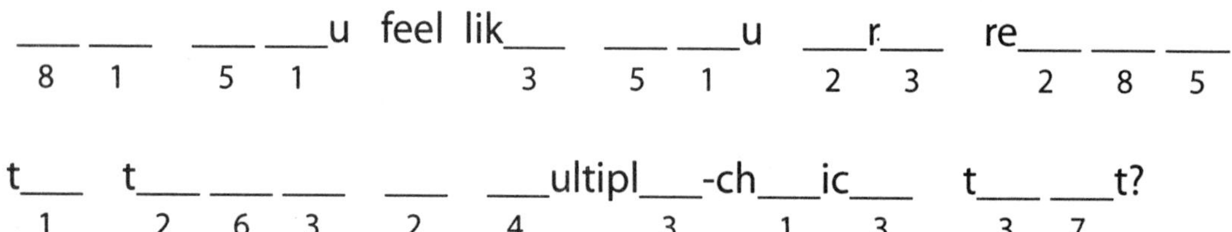

___ ___ ___ ___u feel lik___ ___ ___u ___r___ re___ ___ ___
8 1 5 1 3 5 1 2 3 2 8 5
t___ t___ ___ ___ ___ ___ultipl___-ch___ic___ t___ ___t?
1 2 6 3 2 4 3 1 3 3 7

Name ____________________

True-or-False Tests

True-or-false tests ask you to recognize information and make judgments about the information. It's important to study hard for true-or-false tests.

Directions

Read the statements below. Circle the letter under *True* if a statement is true and circle the letter under *False* if a statement is false. If your answers are correct, you will circle letters that spell a question vertically.

	Statement	True	False
1	It is important to read the statements very carefully.	I	A
2	True-or-false tests are always easy.	T	S
3	You should never read the directions before beginning.	I	T
4	Absolute words, such as *always, never, only,* and *all*, usually indicate a false statement.	H	F
5	Longer statements are always false.	M	I
6	Flexible words, such as *usually, generally, sometimes, frequently,* and *occasionally,* usually indicate a true statement.	S	A
7	The word *because* often links two true statements in a way that makes the overall statement false.	F	G
8	If asked to write, you should print the words *true* and *false* so there is no mistaking your answer.	U	D
9	It doesn't matter how hard you study for a test.	S	N

Write the question here: ____________________?

Always make a guess on a true-or-false test. You have a 50/50 chance of getting it right!

Name ____________________

Fill-in-the-Blank Tests

Fill-in-the-blank tests ask you to write in answers. Be sure to study key words, their definitions, and their spellings when you study for this kind of test.

Word Bank

once	incorrect	spelling	guess	skip
bank	cross	remaining	clue	

Directions

Read the following statements and the words in the word bank. Fill in the blanks with the correct answers.

1. Ask in advance if the test will give a word __________. If it will not, you know you have to memorize answers word for word.

2. If you are unsure of the __________ of a word, look to see if it is written somewhere in the text to help you.

3. If your answer sounds awkward, it is probably __________.

4. If all else fails, be sure to take a __________. If you leave the blank empty, you are sure to get it wrong.

5. Read the directions carefully to see if an answer can be used more than __________.

6. Read an entire statement before writing an answer; a __________ might be given in the second half of the statement.

7. If the test has a word bank, be sure to __________ out answers as you use them. Then __________ questions you don't know. At the end, go back to the unanswered questions and use the __________ answers.

Form your letters neatly! Misspelled words are technically incorrect, especially if the word can be found in a word bank.

Name ______________________________

Essay Tests

When you take an essay test, you need to remember, organize, and write information in a clear, detailed way.

Directions

Pretend you are the teacher. Read the grading scale below and the essays on page 108. Use the grading scale as a guide to grade each essay.

Grading Scale

2 = well done   1 = satisfactory   0 = poor or not done

It's important to memorize information for essay tests. If you know the questions in advance, write practice essays before the test to see how much of the information you remember.

Grading

0 to 6 = F   7 to 10 = D   11 to 14 = C   15 to 17 = B   18 to 20 = A

Element	Points		
1 The student read the test question carefully and looked for key words, such as *compare, contrast, describe, explain,* and *list*. He or she used the key words as a guide and therefore knew how to answer the question.	0	1	2
2 The student underlined key words in the question and then defined the words in the essay.	0	1	2
3 The student read the directions regarding the length of the essay and followed the guidelines.	0	1	2
4 The student brainstormed information to include in the essay.	0	1	2
5 The student organized the brainstormed information into a simple outline.	0	1	2
6 The student began the essay by restating the question.	0	1	2
7 The student answered the question within the essay.	0	1	2
8 The student wrote a clear, detailed essay using the outline as a guide.	0	1	2
9 The student proofread and edited the essay for content, spelling, grammar, and punctuation.	0	1	2
10 If necessary, the student added visuals, such as a drawing, map, or graph.	0	1	2

Name ______________________________

Directions

Read each essay. Use the grading scale on page 107 to grade each essay. Write the points and grade for each essay in the correct place.

Test Question

Why did the *Titanic* sink? Explain your answer in at least two paragraphs.

Essay # 1

The *Titanic* sank for two major reasons. The first reason the ship sank was because it hit an iceberg. Although the lookouts in the crow's nest sounded an alarm, the officer on the bridge could not steer the ship away from the iceberg in time. The ship did not have a head-on collision with the iceberg, but the iceberg had created a gash in *Titanic*'s starboard bow.

The second reason *Titanic* sunk was because of its construction. In the bottom of the ship, there were several watertight compartments. The *Titanic* could remain afloat only if the first four compartments flooded; any more than that and *Titanic* would sink. Within 20 minutes, the first five compartments were flooded and water was spilling over into the ones that remained. The ship and its passengers didn't have a chance.

For these two reasons, *Titanic*, and over 1,000 men, women, and children, sank into the deep, dark ocean.

Points = ____________ **Grade =** ____________

1,000 died
iceberg
Titanic
alarm
compartments
collision

Why Titanic Sank
A. First Reason
1. hit iceberg
2. could not steer away in time
B.
1.
2.

Test Question

Why did the *Titanic* sink? Explain your answer in at least two paragraphs.

Essay # 2

It hit a big iceberg. The iceberg put a whole in the side of the ship. Then water come into the bottom of the ship and filled up a bunch of watertight compartments. Then it sank.

Points = ____________ **Grade =** ____________

Homework Help

Dear Family Member,

When your child is prepared for homework, studying at home is a lot easier. As a parent, you can help your child get ready for homework with the following quick and easy organization tips.

Have enough supplies.

Just as you need the right ingredients for a recipe or the right tools to tune up the car, your child needs the right "tools" to complete his or her homework. Take your child shopping at the beginning of the school year and stock up on paper, pencils, notebooks, and other essentials. Then have your child check his or her supplies periodically so you can replenish the supplies when needed.

Have a designated study area.

Help your child find a spot in the house that can be his or her study area. Be sure the study area is free from distractions and has plenty of light.

Talk about homework with your child.

Be sure your child shows you his or her homework before and after it is completed. Before your child begins, answer any questions he or she might have about completing the assignment. When there are more than two assignments, help your child prioritize the order in which he or she should complete them. When your child asks questions during homework, offer help, but don't give the answers. Provide clues to steer your child in the right direction. After the homework is complete, check to make sure it is done correctly. You can help your child study for tests by asking review questions.

Perhaps the most important thing you can do to help your child become a better student is show him or her that you value education. Read, have conversations with your child, and keep mentally active yourself. When you are a good role model for education, your child will want to learn and do well in school.

Time Management

Dear Family Member,

Adults in college and the business world are often offered time-management courses to help them juggle the many demands on their time. But adults aren't the only ones with a lot to do; children today are asked to do more than ever. The following are some easy things you can do to help your child become a more effective, more efficient time manager.

Carefully look at your child's schedule.

Consider the demands on your child's time. Is your child in several clubs or activities that take time away from studying or family commitments? Does your child have no free time? Consider your child's schedule and help him or her eliminate activities that get in the way of "important" things.

Help your child prioritize.

Talk about time with your child and stress the importance of having enough time to complete tasks well. Show your child how to make prioritized to-do lists that itemize tasks for home as well as school.

Help your child keep a calendar.

Give your child a calendar as a gift. Help him or her record information on the calendar, such as homework due dates, test dates, meeting dates, practice dates, and birthdays. Go over the calendar once a week with your child so he or she knows what is coming up.

The best way to describe your role is that of time-management "coach." Do your best to be available to your child when he or she needs help in planning a schedule. Being there to guide and coach is probably the best way to help your child become a great time manager.

Answer Key

p. 20
17 mistakes.

Thousands of beautiful creatures live and thrive under the sea. Among the many fascinating fish is one called the Red Firefish. This fish has poisonous spines on its back that protect it from other fish.

Another interesting fish is the Triggerfish. It has orange and purple stripes that make it look much larger than it really is. That is what keeps other fish from attacking.

Butterflyfish have dark spots on their tails that look like eyes. This is confusing to other fish that think the head is actually where the tail should be.

The sea is full of wonderful creatures. These three fish are no exception.

p. 38
1) D **2)** E **3)** T **4)** E **5)** C **6)** T **7)** I **8)** V **9)** E
Message: Are you a good detective?

p. 39
Main Idea for Paragraph One:
Spain owned and had power over much of the New World.
Main Idea for Paragraph Two:
Cuba wanted its independence.
Main Idea for Paragraph Three:
The U.S. government sent the *Maine* to protect the Cubans in case of riot.
Main Idea for Paragraph Four:
The *Maine* was destroyed by an underwater explosion, which caused a war with Spain over Cuba's independence.

p. 40
1) title **2)** Review, pictures **3)** throughout, questions
4) key **5)** beginning, summary
6) carefully, meaning, again, missed

p. 43
1) Missouri. **2)** Yes. Accept answers such as *Scanning was easier because it took less time.* **3)** Accept answers such as *Scanning would be helpful during a textbook reading assignment.*

p. 45
1) Albert Einstein was brilliant, but he was a poor student.
2) Accept answers such as *German, Munich, mathematics,* and *intelligence.* **3)** Accept answers such as *Skimming would be helpful when I search for a name in the telephone book.*

p. 51
1) Gila monsters can grow up to two feet long.
2) Yes. **3)** Gila monsters eat rodents, young birds, and eggs. **4)** Gila monsters lay their eggs in a sandy hole.

p. 55
1) F **2)** T **3)** F **4)** T **5)** T **6)** T **7)** F

p. 58
Title: Tyrannosaurus Rex
- I. Body
  - A. Size
    - **1)** Up to 18 feet (5.6 m) high
    - **2)** Up to 50 feet (15 m) long
  - B. Body Adaptations
    - **1)** 3-foot (90-cm) jaws with 60 sharp teeth
    - **2)** 2 long, strong, clawed legs and 2 short arms
- II. Reproduction
  - A. Eggs
    - **1)** Eggs were proportionately smaller in size compared to bird eggs
    - **2)** Up to 15 eggs in one grouping
  - B. Nests
    - **1)** Crater-like holes dug next to streams
    - **2)** Holes the size of the diameter of the mother's body
- III. Habitat
  - A. Regions
    - **1)** Western North America
    - **2)** Mongolia
  - B. Environmental Conditions
    - **1)** Warmer temperatures than today
    - **2)** Fewer plant and animal species

pp. 62 and 63
1) English **2)** a favorite summer memory
3) in one week **4)** d. narrative **5)** four minutes
6) b. note cards **7)** a. yes **8)** d. chalkboard **9)** a. yes
10) no bibliography needed

p. 65
1) g **2)** d **3)** e **4)** a **5)** f **6)** c **7)** b **8)** h

pp. 70 and 71
1) reading **2)** a favorite athlete **3)** in two weeks
4) c. handwritten or typed **5)** b. single spaced with a double space between paragraphs **6)** e. bottom center of the page **7)** a. yes **8)** a. yes **9)** a. yes **10)** at least two

Answer Key

p. 73
1) glad, pleased, delighted **2)** Green Bay Packers
3) \ser-ə-be-ləm\ **4)** approximately 120,000
5) Southeastern Africa **6)** Jody Williams **7)** Accept answers such as *Water is let into ballast tanks until the submarine sinks to the desired depth.* **8)** Europe **9)** huge
10) egg, larva (caterpillar), pupa (cocoon or chrysalis), adult

p. 76
Title: Elizabeth Blackwell

- I. Accomplishments
  - A. Why Important
    - **1)** Became first woman to receive a medical degree in the U.S.
  - B. How She Helped Others
    - **1)** Wrote papers on the importance of good hygiene
    - **2)** Opened an infirmary especially for women and children
    - **3)** Established the Women's Medical College of New York in 1868
- II. Childhood
  - A. Birth
    - **1)** Born in Bristol, England
    - **2)** In 1821
  - B. Where She Lived
    - **1)** Moved to New York in 1832, to New Jersey in 1835, and to Ohio in 1838
    - **2)** Stayed in Ohio until she got a teaching job in Kentucky
- III. Education
  - A. Elementary School
    - **1)** In England until she was 11
    - **2)** In New York City until she was 12
  - B. Secondary School
    - **1)** At home with her mother as teacher
  - C. College
    - **1)** Accepted to Geneva College in 1848
    - **2)** La Maternité in Paris, France
    - **3)** St. Bartholomew School of Medicine in England
- IV. Challenges
  - A. Challenges from Others
    - **1)** Was turned down by several medical schools including Harvard
    - **2)** No institution in the United States would hire her after she got her M.D.
  - B. Physical Challenges
    - **1)** Contracted ophthalmia, an eye infection that blinded one eye
    - **2)** Fell in 1907, never recovered, and died in 1910 as a result

p. 79
Across:
1) bibliography **4)** word **6)** handwriting **7)** title **9)** mistakes
Down:
2) read **3)** computer **5)** indent **8)** label

p. 95

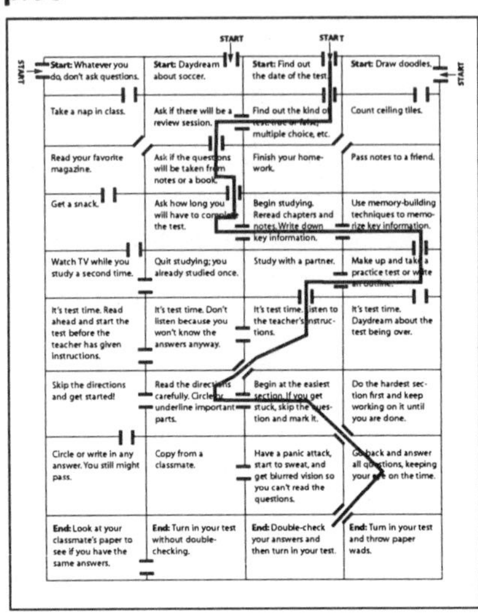

p. 100
1) Arizona's state flower is the Giant Cactus. **2)** Line 1: no, Line 2: yes. **3)** *Moon* should have one line. *Shone* should have two lines. **4)** clearly **5)** 1. weak b. 2. week a.

p. 101
Only the directions for steps 3, 4, and 10 should be recorded.

p. 102
486 + 359 = 845; 845 – 359 = 486
1,463 – 858 = 605; 605 + 858 = 1,463
885 x 9 = 7,965; 7,965 ÷9 = 885

p. 103
1) G **2)** O **3)** F **4)** O **5)** R **6)** I **7)** T
Sentence: Go for it!

p. 104
1) o **2)** a **3)** e **4)** m **5)** y **6)** k **7)** s **8)** d
Sentence: Do you feel like you are ready to take a multiple-choice test?

p. 105
1) I **2)** S **3)** T **4)** H **5)** I **6)** S **7)** F **8)** U
9) N Question: Is this fun?

p. 106
1) bank **2)** spelling **3)** incorrect **4)** guess
5) once **6)** clue **7)** cross, skip, remaining